HIDDEN HISTORY *of* TOLEDO

Lou Hebert

THE History PRESS

Published by The History Press
Charleston, SC
www.historypress.com

First published 2019

Manufactured in the United States

ISBN 9781467140294

Library of Congress Control Number: 2018960970

Contents

Preface

The narrative of Toledo's rise from the depths of the Black Swamp to that of a key industrial city of the Midwest has been told many times before over many decades. This is not new. Consequently, the tapestry of that history is often a well-worn pattern of the same characters and story lines that is familiar to most. In *Hidden History of Toledo*, my attempt was to search out those narratives that were perhaps not as well known—the colorful or interesting stories and people that have gone largely unreported, tucked away and lost in the shadowy corners of memory and time. Finding those pearls and revealing them is a great joy, and so it's been a labor of great passion to spend countless hours researching and reading countless old newspapers where many of the forgotten old tales still live. Thankfully, there are many others who share my love for the past, and they have offered abundant help for this effort in many forms, from personal experiences to professional encouragement. These include Nan Card, Clark Curtis, Ken and Bonnie Dickson, Shirley Green, John Jaeger, Judy Justus, Peter Mintun, Leo Schnapp, Mike Tailford, Doug Tracy and all those nameless newspaper scribes of years past who chronicled the players and events that remain forever frozen in ink.

Special thanks to the *Toledo Blade* photo department; the Toledo Police Museum; the Ward Canaday Center for Special Collections at the University of Toledo; the U.S. Postal Service Museum at the Smithsonian Institution; the Ottawa County Historical Society, Port Clinton, Ohio; the Toledo–Lucas County Public Library's local history section; the Perrysburg Public Library;

the Wood County Public Library; the Ohio State Historical Society; the Rutherford B. Hayes Presidential Library; the U.S. Consul office in Quebec, Canada; the Harness Racing Museum, Goshen, New York; the Franklin County Records and Research Center, Ottawa, Kansas; the Storis Museum; and the U.S. Coast Guard.

Most of all, I'd like to hug my wonderful spouse, Kay-Lynne, who has been a tolerant and patient "history widow" through this project and yet still likes me. I'd also like to thank my dear mom and dad, who spent scores of Ohio Sunday afternoons dragging me and my brother to visit history museums, monuments, random historical signage or other sundry roadside attractions of some historical merit. I didn't know it at the time, but they gave us something money could never buy.

Chapter 1

Cresceus

The Great Horse

It was the spring of 1894 when, on the horse farm of Toledo's highly respected and wealthy Ketcham family, a young colt was foaled. It was an awkward sorrel that stumbled around the stall box and didn't seem to possess the qualities of fine horses that were often brought to life and prominence on this farm located along what is now Alexis Road in the Trilby area. The superintendent of the Ketcham Farm, Fred Murnen, kept his apprising eye on the clumsy colt that was trying to reach his mother or "dam," Mabel, but couldn't quite reach. Murnen said to another man in the barn, "Well, he might not be good-looking, but he might grow up to be a good horse someday."

As weeks and months went by, the colt grew to be a large and stout horse with long legs. He did not have the look of champions, but he was a good, solid horse. As a yearling, the colt developed some blisters on his throat and, in trying to scratch them, rubbed his neck against a stall frame and rubbed so hard that he opened the flesh, exposing his windpipe. It was a hideous sight, and George Ketcham, the owner of the farm, told Murnen that perhaps it would be best to have him killed, as the horse would be of little use to them. Murnen, though, wanted to give the ugly duckling colt another chance and allowed him to live. He took him to the back pastures and let him heal, out of sight of Ketcham. Soon, Murnen began to see some promise in the big stallion. After all, the sire of the horse was McGregor, the notorious mean-tempered champion that was well regarded despite his vile reputation. He was so mean, it was said, that "he never met a man he didn't want to kill."

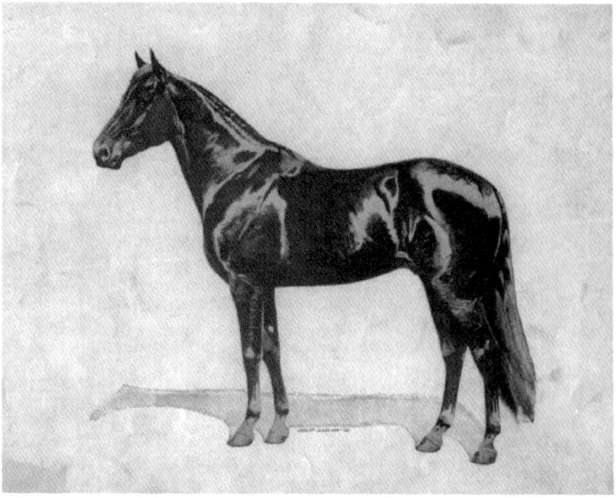

Cresceus, Toledo's most famous horse.

It appeared that he may have passed down some of that ornery disposition to this colt, for this young horse was also reported to be hot tempered and full of fire, and best of all, he wanted to run. After being broken to the harness, the colt was finally revealed and presented to Ketcham. He was told that the horse he almost had killed had the makings of a great trotter. Ketcham began to train this colt and named it Crescens for the famous and fast charioteer of Roman legend. The first time Crescens was taken out on a course over the snow paths of Toledo as a two-year-old, he put his head down and trotted. Ketcham and Murnen quickly noted that he had natural speed and gave them a pleasant surprise when he trotted past one of the fastest horses in the Toledo area.

The two horsemen knew they had something special and took their time in training the colt. Their patience and care paid off. They wanted to allow his muscles to harden and develop without being strained. Racing only a few times as a two-year-old, he won one of them and came in second in the others. He continued his regimen of training, and then as a three-year-old, he was racing again and winning. If he did not get first place, he was in the top three finishers. During the winter of his third year, Ketcham put him on the snow tracks regularly, and the stallion was so fast and won so many races that he began to develop a reputation among other horsemen of Toledo and the area. It was obvious to most that he was more than fast. He was a likely champion. His gait, his endurance and his speed were admired by all as he continued to win and set new records. For the next six years, Crescens—who would be renamed Cresceus, not intentionally, but because of a printer's error in a racing form—ran with the best horses and continued to earn championship honors. No matter what he was

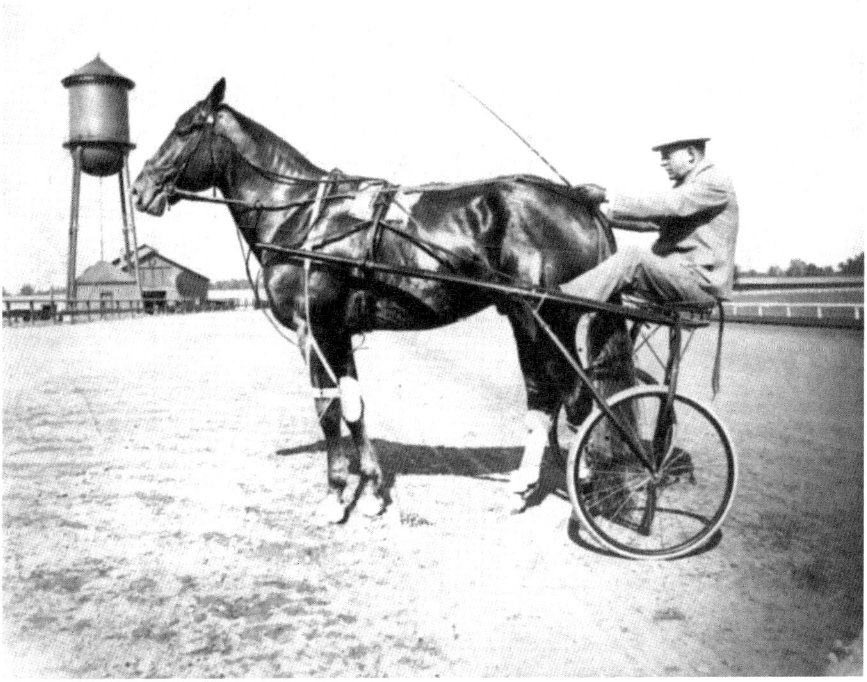

Cresceus and owner George Katchem in Toledo. *Courtesy of Harness Racing Museum, Goshen, New York.*

called, people in Toledo loved him. They were Cresceus crazy, as the big and broad chestnut stallion had captured the heart of the public. Special appearances and events were held in Toledo and across the nation. Fans would turn out by the thousands just for a glimpse of the stallion that was becoming a legend.

At the end of a brilliant season of racing for Cresceus and his owner, George Ketcham, in 1900, Cresceus returned to Toledo for a hero's welcome. On October 12, 1900, as a special rail car opened its doors, Cresceus stepped out to cheers and applause. Then a jubilant parade to Ketcham's home on Cherry Street commenced. Accompanied by a bugle corps and four companies of the Sixteenth Regiment, thousands of people joined the march. It was a mix of people from all walks of life—letter carriers, street rail workers, office workers, mothers and children, a drill squad called the Cherry Pickers and several bands and carriages. They walked Toledo's streets at dusk, which were lined with applauding fans and citizens who were very proud of this Toledo horse called Cresceus. Once the procession reached Ketcham's house, he announced to the crowd:

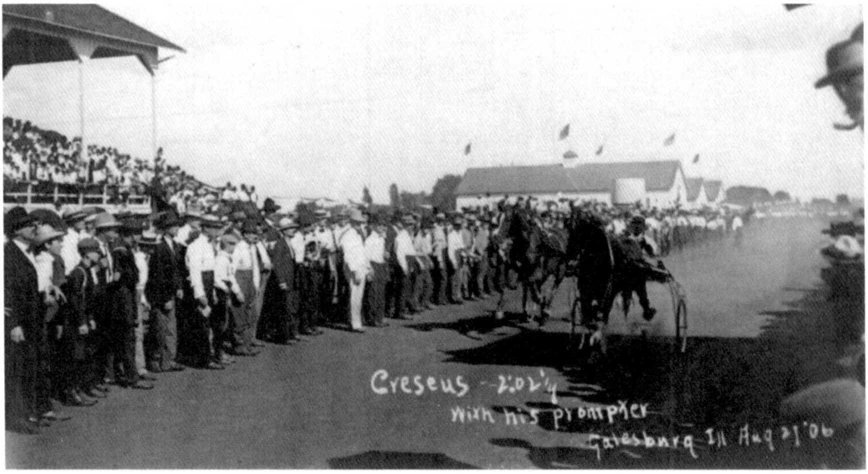

A postcard depicts crowds lining the track to get a glimpse of Cresceus. *Courtesy of Harness Racing Museum, Goshen, New York.*

> *Fellow Townsmen, I do not know what to say or how to say it. For once I am overpowered with emotion and my voice is shaky. I know this demonstration is in large part in appreciation of the greatest horse that ever lived. This is made more satisfactory to me and you when it is taken into consideration that Cresceus is a product of Toledo. He was raised here and trained here in Toledo and has upheld the honor and dignity of the city by beating the fastest horses of the world.*

The next day, even more honors and adoration of the great horse came from the hearts of Toledoans, as they turned out at the fairgrounds for a special exhibition of the Cresceus speed. Spectators watched in jubilation as Cresceus pulled the sulky with Ketcham aboard, to a blazing time of 2.09¾, lowering the track record for the mile and lowering the world record for the half mile. An ovation of cheers could be heard throughout the city.

At this point, the chestnut stallion's all-time record for a mile was 2.04, the world's fastest mile for a stallion trotter. But Ketcham and Murnen wanted to see if they could beat that time and become the fastest of any horse.

The next year, 1901, would surpass all expectations. As a stallion, Cresceus was the fastest and in a class by himself. But not for long. On July 26, under a cloudless summer sky at the Glenville race track in Cleveland, on the first race of the day, Cresceus, a seven-year-old, would stun the crowd. Hundreds jumped to their feet in awe at the speed of the horse. Many wondered if this

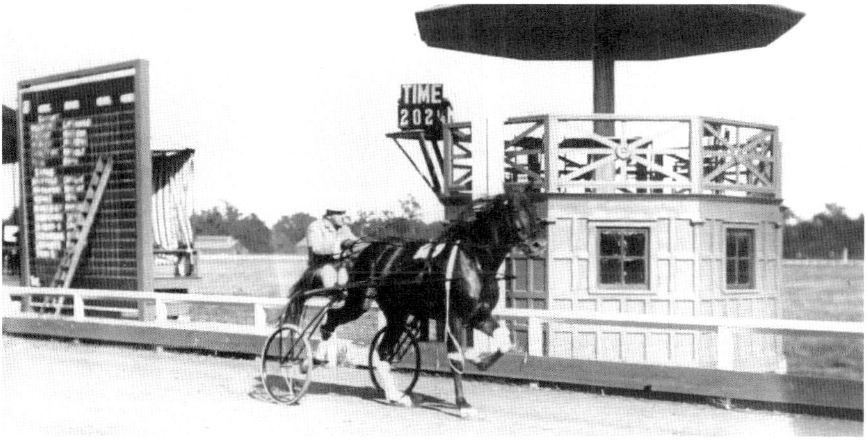

Cresceus in action on the track. *Courtesy of Harness Racing Museum, Goshen, New York.*

big stallion could run so fast without falling. But steady and sure, thundering around the oval, with Toledo's George Ketcham driving, Cresceus put his nose across the wire at an amazing 2.02¾ for the mile—a new world record, for any horse. When news of the feat traveled around the globe, Cresceus was dubbed the "Monarch of the Mile."

Cresceus must have liked running on Ohio tracks, because about a week later, the great horse was taken to Columbus. It was a cool and windy day with a few drops of rain, and George Ketcham had no expectations that Cresceus could beat his record from the week before, especially given the nasty weather. But the big stallion must have had other ideas. After a few trial runs of average times, the moment was at hand for the real attempt. Fifteen thousand fans who were there to see the world's best trotters got to witness history. Cresceus would blaze around the track, nose against the wind, moving at lightning speed, and finish the mile by beating the record he had set a week before with 2.02¼. It was racing history, and Cresceus carved his place on the list of racing legends for all time. He had become the undisputed champion of champions.

Yet another major celebration was held for Cresceus in Toledo after his incredible performance year of 1901. Ketcham requested that Cresceus Day be declared on October 11, as he wanted to thank the citizens of Toledo for their undying support of the big, fast horse. An exhibition was to be held for the public, charging only twenty-five cents a person so that no one would be prevented from seeing the champion. Ketcham vowed that all the money raised would go to the charities of Toledo to help the poor of Lucas County.

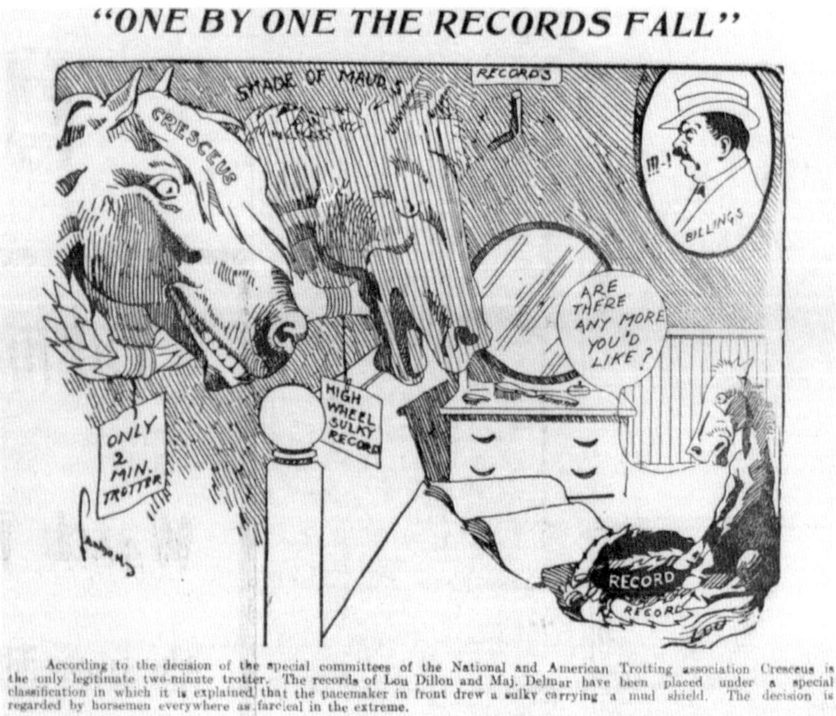
"ONE BY ONE THE RECORDS FALL"

According to the decision of the special committees of the National and American Trotting association Cresceus is the only legitimate two-minute trotter. The records of Lou Dillon and Maj. Delmar have been placed under a special classification in which it is explained that the pacemaker in front drew a sulky carrying a mud shield. The decision is regarded by horsemen everywhere as farcical in the extreme.

Newspaper cartoon featuring Cresceus as a "record breaker."

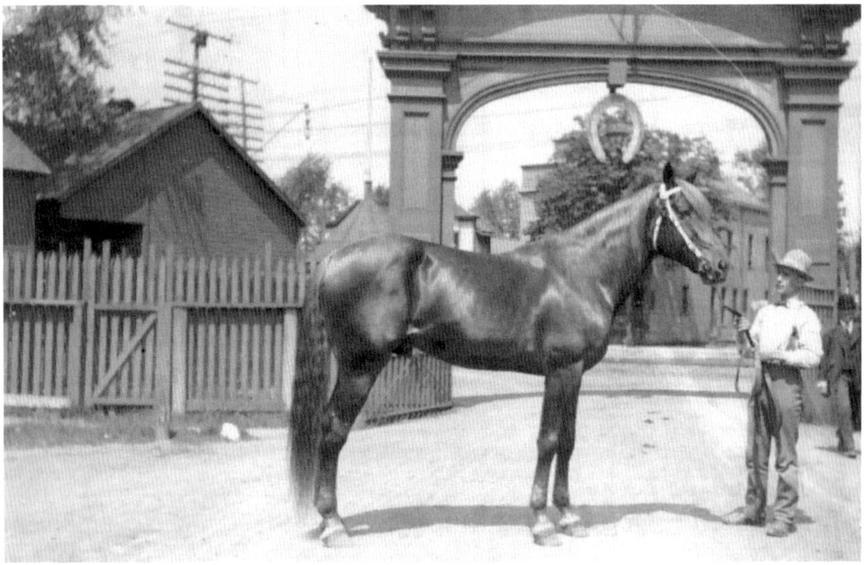

Cresceus posing with trainer Ed Mitchell. *Courtesy of Harness Racing Museum, Goshen, New York.*

Major Sam Jones agreed with the request, so on Friday, October 11, it seemed as though all of northwestern Ohio and southeastern Michigan was turning out to see the noble champion. The streets were alive with people and carriages, and every streetcar was packed to capacity. Their destination was the fairground on Stickney Avenue. George Ketcham stood proudly in front of the packed grandstands and was greeted by Mayor Jones, who congratulated Ketcham and thanked him for this charitable event. It was then that Ketcham revealed why he had selected October 11 as the special day: it was his mother's birthday. His face grew serious as he told the crowd, "She is eighty years old today. When she came here in 1835, all of this country was wilderness. She was the daughter of the first mayor of Toledo [John Berdan]. My efforts today are her contribution to charity on her eightieth birthday as a manifestation for the good health and prosperity she has enjoyed in this community."

The city was touched by Ketcham's remarks. More than twenty thousand people had attended the event, and many felt this had been a historic day, which raised over $4,300 for the charities of the community. It was an impressive sum in those years and inspired others to give large amounts in the name of Cresceus. The brilliant career of Toledo's Monarch of the Mile was not over. He would still run many more races, impressing his adoring fans from coast to coast, but he would never have another year like 1901.

Ketcham would write later about Cresceus, saying he was a horse "with striking individuality and peculiar characteristics." He praised the stallion's ability to work with the driver and his trainers and claimed that he really was "easy to handle," despite stories that he was ugly, difficult and mean. Ketcham said, "He is very even tempered and his habits are as methodical as a traditional old maid." But he did write that Cresceus was not one to make friends and didn't like to be touched by strangers. "To his trainers and those who are in charge of him, though, he has a lovable disposition and an interest in them that is remarkable." The proud owner also talked of the horse's ability to never let new surroundings or annoyances bother him, which Ketcham said is rare among horses or anyone—singer, actor, orator or anyone who has ever achieved fame.

Many may not know that Cresceus hated "stable dogs" and didn't want them around him, but in his later years, a friend introduced a bull terrier to Cresceus. For some reason, the horse took a liking to this handsome dog, and the two of them became fast friends. The dog was hence named Cresceus Jr., "The Mascot."

It was always assumed that George Ketcham would never part with the great horse and he would be allowed to grow old gracefully in the pastures

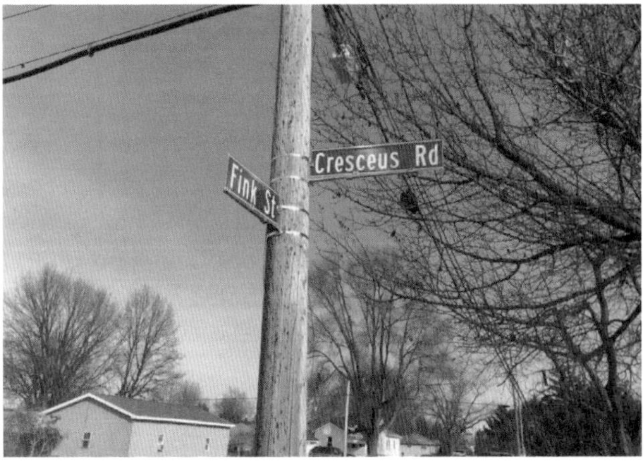

A quiet street in East Toledo is the only visible legacy left in the city of the great horse. *Author's collection.*

of the famed West Toledo farm. In 1903, he was retired to stud after winning more than $120,000 in his lifetime. But then, in 1905, Ketcham parted with Cresceus, who was sold for $21,000 to M.S. Savage, the owner of Dan Patch, another famous harness racer of the day. Savage held him for a few years in Minnesota and then sold him to a wealthy Russian businessman who wanted to improve the bloodline of his equestrian stock. It is said that Cresceus did not like his new surroundings, his new country or his new owner, who would often use the noble champ as a mere workhorse for transportation, pulling his sleigh to the taverns in the dead of the cold Russian winters. The Russian, though, soon tired of showing off his American conquest and sent him to a stock farm to stud. Cresceus lived for a few years after that, but not for long. He would pass into the memory of mortals in the year 1915, at the age of twenty-one.

The memory of Cresceus, however, is not a strong one today in Toledo—or anywhere, with the exception of among horse racing historians. The name and triumphs of the big chestnut stallion have mostly faded and been forgotten in northwestern Ohio. The Ketcham farm is long gone, its pastures now filled with the homes and streets of West Toledo. But one of those streets and even a school are named McGregor, the name of the ill-tempered sire to Cresceus. Only in the Toledo suburb of Oregon will you find a street named for the great horse Cresceus. It is a short residential stretch of roadway with no relevance to racing. However, adjacent to Cresceus Street are the streets of Dan Patch and Mambrino, also harness racing legends in their day. Other than these few tokens of homage, little remains to remind us of Cresceus, the great horse that made Toledo proud.

Chapter 2

Dell Hair

Toledo's Famous Cop Poet

Cops who put down their pistols and pick up pens in the gentle pursuit of poetry may seem like a rare breed, but perhaps they're not as rare as you might think. The need to express oneself affects people from all modes of life, and police officers who see the world from a different angle than most of us frequently like to tell their stories—sometimes in narrative, sometimes in song, sometimes in artistic verse. Whether it's the constant conflict with the criminal elements, the nagging fear of the night or close exposure to life's raw emotion, these poignant moments often serve to inspire the inner poet of the cop. A quick search of the Internet today will produce myriad such rhymes and ballads created by a growing army of police-poets.

It's very likely that one of the first policemen to aim his pen at a sheet of paper to reveal his inner thoughts as he strolled the beat was Dell Hair, a Toledo policeman. He was the nation's first cop-poet, or at least the first one who was nationally recognized for his verse. While not considered a great poet, Dell was popular and was published numerous times in the course of a career that included walking the dark streets of downtown Toledo, fighting crime while composing rhyme.

He was born Adalbert Hair on a farm near the small Michigan town of Morrice, near Lansing, on November 4, 1871. His father, Joseph, was a blacksmith, and his mother, Mary, was the daughter of a lawyer in nearby Howell, Michigan. He had a brother who was a good student and a minister, but Dell was not one to be tied to the labor of education. He was said to have a "wild" side, and when he was small, he captured a turtle, harnessed it and trained it. He was considered so "weird" by the standards of the day that he was often referred to as "Joe Hair's Fool." But Dell was not to be discouraged, for his love of nature and his affinity for writing lyrical verse would last a lifetime. It is said that when some townspeople would insult him to his face, they might awaken the next day to find a note of verse on their doorstep in answer to their insult. Dell eventually abandoned his formal education, and his father put him to work on a plow. It was work he abhorred, so much so that sometimes he would stop in the middle of the furrow and write a couplet or two about how much he hated it. And thus, he wrote one day:

The farm was just a present
To stay doth me behoove
Did I not love my neighbor
I'd shoot these mules and move.

As soon as he could, at nineteen, Dell did move. He packed his grips, took his drum and headed for Detroit, where he enlisted in the army, asking to be given the most dangerous assignment they had. That's how he got sent to Oklahoma's Fort Sill, where he was made a drummer boy in the Thirteenth Infantry Regiment.

His service in those years also included time spent with the Third Cavalry, which was stationed along the Mexican border for a time, where his unit caught the notorious Mexican bandit Biena Vidies. At Fort Sill, Dell recalls having spent numerous stints in the guardhouse for infractions of military rules, or disobeying orders. While confined to the brig, he would write more poetry or play his drum. In the same guardhouse was the notorious Apache renegade legend Geronimo, who likely heard Dell play the drum many times.

An elegy written by Dell Hair in the Fort Sill guardhouse starts like this:

All wrapt in darkness sleeps the world
And in the cell where I lay
All light, all peace tonight is furled
The paint cup fadeth not away
The thrush has stilled his merry song
The beetle too has taken flight
The screech owl to her nest has gone
Bats complain of the starless night.

My officers I now disdain
Their laws I did rebel
Now centipedes with me complain
Of the mouldy dismal cell.

Hair eventually left the army and made his way back to the Midwest and to Toledo, where, in 1906, he joined the ranks of the Toledo Police Department. This, of course, was long before squad cars, so Hair spent much of his time on foot as a patrolman. While he was on duty, it is reported that he not only worked out poems in his head but often gave those suspects he arrested on-the-spot renditions of his verse as he hauled them back to the police station. From those many days and nights on the streets, in 1908, he published a collection of poems that he wrote, titled *Echoes from the Beat.*

About a year later, Hair left the Toledo Police Department, under controversial circumstances, and formed his own downtown private security company, which was really a poetic way of saying he hired out as a night watchman to check on downtown stores. But he did it well and did it for many years until he died, all the while writing and publishing his poems and even becoming involved in city politics. A *Toledo New Bee* article in 1909 reports that Dell Hair spoke to a political rally in a campaign against then Toledo mayor Brand Whitlock, in which Hair claimed he was fired by the police department because Whitlock, also a writer, was "jealous of his literary accomplishments." Hair was not shy about voicing his opinions and was outspoken on many issues of the times, often putting those concerns about city problems into iambic pentameter. He was also a favorite character with many in the city, especially the downtown merchants whose stores he protected at night. Hair even tried running for mayor in Toledo in 1915 but returned to his police work and his poetry. Dell Hair lived at 1005 Salem Street in Toledo and was married to his wife, Charlotte, with whom he had several children. He continued writing poetry and stayed on the downtown beat until his death from the flu in 1932.

During his lifetime, he wrote and published many books of poetry, many of which are still available on eBay and other used book sites. Some of the titles to look for are *Roses and Thorns*, published while he was in the army; *Songs of Darkness, Light and Death* from 1895; *Nature Beautiful*, published in 1929; and *Violets and Thorns* and *Echoes from a Dell*, published in 1922. Dell Hair was described by those who knew him as a large man in stature, a big and burly guy who, despite his love of poetry, always put his respect and admiration first for his fellow officers and firemen. His

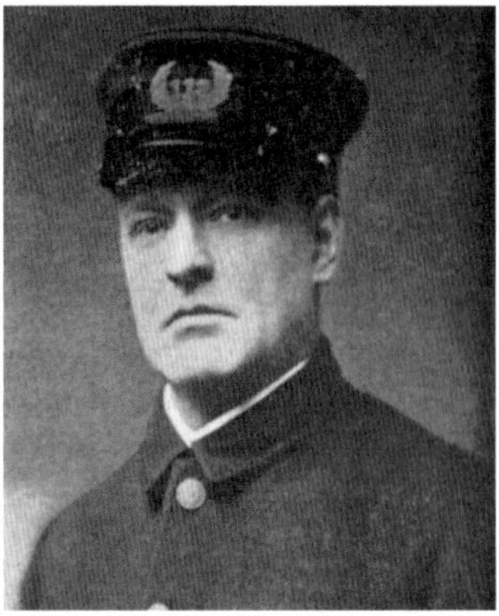

Echoes from the Beat was a book of poems that focused on Officer Hair's police experiences. *Courtesy Toledo Police Museum.*

books of poetry ranged in topic from law enforcement to nature and human nature. His books also include many Toledo-themed topics and even some local drawings and photos.

Exactly what motivated Dell Hair to be a cop and writer of poetry, we'll probably never know for sure; maybe he didn't know either. But Jessee Fourmy, a latter-day poet-cop in Los Angeles, believes it has to do with a cop's natural instinct to study and understand human nature. He says they are seekers of truth, which is also the goal of the poet. Fourmy says there are so many cops now writing poetry on the West Coast that they have started their own journal called *Rattle*, in which former Portland police officer turned poet James Fleming writes, "Cops and poets are intruders into other people's lives. They both probe for character, motive, history. They both want to know what people are up to. A person of interest can end up in a poem or in jail."

And a police poem can end up in an editorial. In fact, the *Toledo Blade* used one of Dell Hair's old poems in 1964 when controversy arose over the old Spielbusch Fountain at the Civic Center at Spielbusch and Cherry Streets. The decaying old stone structure was destined to be torn down, despite the cries of those who wanted to save it. The *Blade* proposed that a marker be erected near the site of the fountain with a poem from Dell Hair, in which he waxed profoundly about how the fountain not only quenched his physical thirst but also satisfied his muse of inspiration. This from "Echoes from the Beat":

Old beautiful fountain so holy and good, adorning the place where the old market stood.
Where mammoth iron bars were bolted in rows, Where horses fought flies now a green carpet grows.
Thy dome is not lofty, thy cups are not gold, The people here flock like sheep to the fold.
Mothers to children, for pitchers will call, There is plenty to spare and enough for us all

On every morn between three and four, I quench my thirst from thy bountiful store
As in the tin cup, I thy purity view, A short little verse is whispered for you
Oh beautiful fountain this is my song of the memory erected to one that is gone
All thanks to the son who lowered the rod, that brought to the people one blessing of god.

To this writer's knowledge, that marker was never placed at the site, and the Spielbusch Fountain is long gone. But the words of poet-policeman Dell Hair live on. He likely will outlive all of us as his verse is passed from generation to generation, perhaps a little dusty with time, but still there, to drink in, like a fountain that just keeps flowing.

Chapter 3

Perrysburg's Clara Blinn

Tragedy on the Plains

The colorful American West is a seductive place. Its broad rocky shoulders and yawning open plains have always, over the decades, lured dreamers to its untamed frontier—a frontier that holds the promise of a richer life, be it gold, land or just the freedom to start life anew. Most often, those early pioneers who were captivated by its magnetism were those who had earlier established new lives in the fledgling hamlets and cities of the Midwest in Pennsylvania, Indiana, Michigan, Iowa and Ohio. But the roots of romance are often restless. We see that in the thousands of pioneers who opted to follow their hearts as they followed the wagon ruts of others before them, braving the crucible of plain and prairie in search of a better life.

Such was the case of Elmore, Ohio native Clara Blinn. Born as Clara Isabel Harrington in 1847 to one of the earliest pioneer families in Ottawa County, she would later move with her family to Perrysburg in Wood County, where her father ran the Baird House Hotel. When the petite and pretty Clara Harrington was nineteen years of age, she met and married Richard Foote Blinn of Perrysburg in 1865. The following year, their life together was blessed with a young boy, William. Their life in Perrysburg was by all accounts a happy one. The freckle-faced, beautiful young Clara sang in a local Methodist church choir and exhibited a good sense of humor and joy. But the western promise beckoned, and the Blinns' dream did not include settling down in the small community along the Maumee River for the rest of their lives. By 1868, the itch to move was too great, so they and other

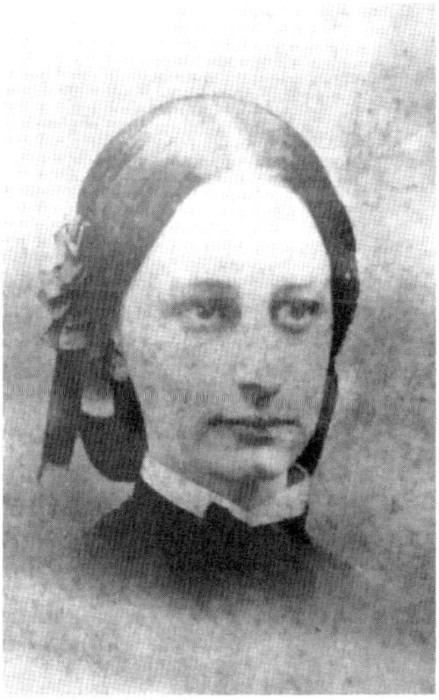

Clara Harrington Blinn was born in Elmore and later moved to Perrysburg before heading to the western United States. *Judy Justus Collection.*

Harrington and Blinn family members set out with all their earthly possessions to create a promising new future. Instead of realizing that promise, Clara, Richard and young Willie found themselves caught in the deadly snare of one of the most infamous clashes between the U.S. Cavalry and the Native Americans during the violent Indian Wars of the Great Plains.

The Harrington family and many of the Blinns would settle near the Kansas town of Ottawa in Franklin County. The younger Blinn family, however, desired to go deeper into the Colorado Territory. One of their aims was to find an arid climate for Richard, who had suffered a severe arm wound during the Civil War that never healed right. They believed that a drier climate would help relieve some of the constant pain. Clara, Willie and Richard would eventually find a place in what is now southeastern Colorado, not far from the Arkansas River and the town of Lamar along the old Santa Fe Trail. There they were engaged to run a stage stop about thirty miles west of the Kansas border. But the yawning and bleak eastern prairies of Colorado offered little in the way of comfort or hope. Within months, the Blinns found they were barely able to eke out an existence on the sunbaked hard pan of the high desert plains. The climate and land were nothing like the verdant and fertile abundance they had left behind along the banks of the Maumee River at Perrysburg. Homesick to see their families, by the late summer of 1868, Clara and Richard decided they had little choice but to load up their supplies and join an eastward wagon train that would return them to a gentler life in the town of Ottawa, Kansas, where Clara and Richard had family. The wagon train was composed of eight wagons, a herd of cattle and ten men. Clara and Willie were placed in the supply wagon.

The entourage set out on their eastward trek, but on October 8, not far from Fort Lyons, near the Kansas border, the wagon train was met by a band of about seventy-five Indians, believed to be Cheyenne, who had been watching and tracking the wagons' every move. Their attack began right

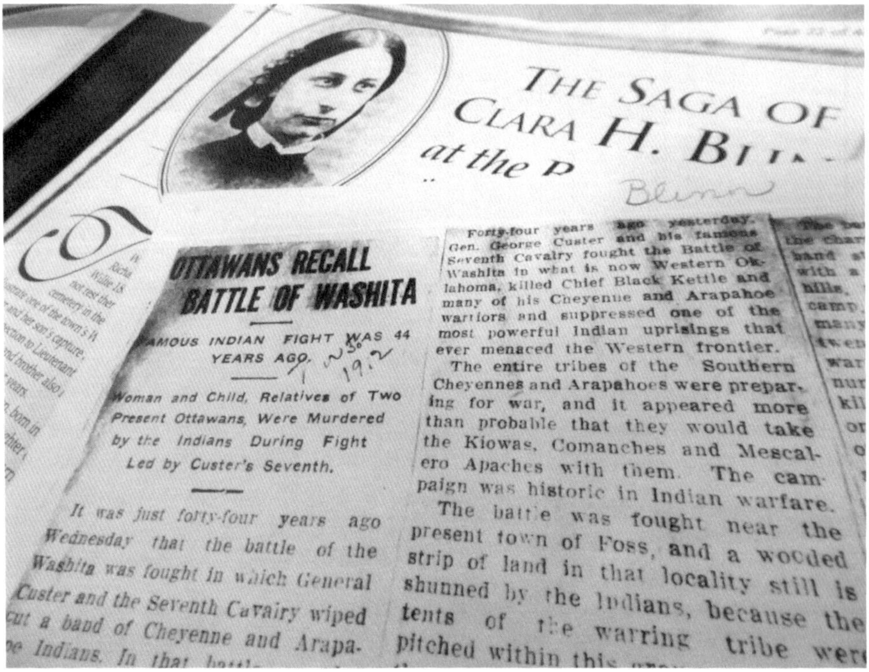

The Saga of Clara H. B...
at the P...
Blinn

OTTAWANS RECALL BATTLE OF WASHITA

FAMOUS INDIAN FIGHT WAS 44 YEARS AGO.

Woman and Child, Relatives of Two Present Ottawans, Were Murdered by the Indians During Fight Led by Custer's Seventh.

It was just forty-four years ago Wednesday that the battle of the Washita was fought in which General Custer and the Seventh Cavalry wiped out a band of Cheyenne and Arapahoe Indians. In that batt...

Forty-four years ago yesterday Gen. George Custer and his famous Seventh Cavalry fought the Battle of Washita in what is now Western Oklahoma, killed Chief Black Kettle and many of his Cheyenne and Arapahoe warriors and suppressed one of the most powerful Indian uprisings that ever menaced the Western frontier.

The entire tribes of the Southern Cheyennes and Arapahoes were preparing for war, and it appeared more than probable that they would take the Kiowas, Comanches and Mescalero Apaches with them. The campaign was historic in Indian warfare.

The battle was fought near the present town of Foss, and a wooded strip of land in that locality still is shunned by the Indians, because the tents of the warring tribe were pitched within this...

The Washita Massacre remains a controversial topic in the American West. *Courtesy Franklin County, Kansas Historical Center.*

after the supply wagon carrying Clara and Willie had set out ahead of the others. Once the wagons were divided, the attack commenced. A group of Indians began chasing the supply wagon with Clara and Willie inside and forced them across the Arkansas River. Other Indians—as many as two hundred—joined the attack. This was part of a new insurgency by tribes against the steady influx of new white settlers from the East immigrating into the Indian Territories. These new white settlers were frequently the targets of attacks by bands of Indians who killed and burned them out from Kansas to Colorado. On this day, the Indians circled the small wagon train and shot flaming arrows into the covered wagons. The wagons burned, and underneath the charred rubble of their belongings, the men were pinned down for several days. Some of the men were wounded, including Richard Blinn and a brother-in-law. To Richard's horror, Clara and Willie were nowhere to be seen, presumably captured by the Indians. What might become of them could only be conjured in the darkest corners of his imagination. Those fears took new gravity after the charred remains of the supply wagon were eventually found. His young wife Clara and son

Willie were gone. But found in a bush not far away was a note in the hand of Clara Blinn. It read:

> *Dear Dick, Willie and I are prisoners. They are going to keep us. If you live, save us if you can. We are with them. Dick, if you love us, save us.*
>
> *Clara Blinn*

Richard was inconsolable. A search of the territory near the ambush site did not turn up any other signs of where they might have been taken. Within a few weeks, as the weather began to turn toward winter, the official search for Clara was abandoned.

The brown landscape of the plains country is wide. It stretches as a rolling prairie for hundreds of miles, as far as the eye can see. It is daunting to consider travel across it for days and hundreds of miles, but to the plains Indians, it was their home. For centuries, they roamed the terrain freely and traveled its wild ranges with familiarity. About 250 miles south of where the attack took place is where Chief Black Kettle had already moved his Cheyenne to their wintering grounds, along the banks of the Washita River in what is now the state of Oklahoma. This was where Clara and Willie were being held hostage.

Just what Clara's life and that of her son were like during their time in the camp can only be assumed. A popular belief was that Clara, like most white women held captive by Indians at that time, would suffer the so-called fate worse than death, likely becoming the victim of repeated sexual assaults and degradation. White women were commonly expected to kill themselves rather than face the torment of their "savage" captors. Those women who did not commit suicide but escaped or were set free by the Indians frequently became outcasts in their own families. They would be victimized twice, as they were ostracized and shunned by their white communities upon their return. It was a different time and different moral code. For the feisty Clara Blinn, survival is what she chose, and shortly after being taken hostage, she managed to smuggle a letter out of the Indian camp to a young trader named Cheyenne Jack, pleading that she and her son be saved. It said, in part:

> *Kind Friend,*
>
> *Whoever you may be, I thank you for your kindness to me and my child. You want me to let you know my wishes. If you could buy us from the Indians*

with ponies or anything and let me come and stay with you until I could get word to my friends, they would pay you and I would work and do all that I could for you. If it is not too far from the camp and you are not afraid to come, I pray that you will try. They tell me, as near as I can understand, they expect traders to come and they will sell us to them. Can you find out by this man and let me know if it is a white man. If it is Mexicans, I am afraid they will sell us into slavery into Mexico. If you can do nothing for me, write to W.T. Harrington, my father, in Ottawa, Franklin County, Kansas. Tell him we are with the Cheyenne and they say when white men make peace, we can go home. Tell him to write to the governor of Kansas about it and for them to make peace. Send this to him. We were taken on the ninth of October on the Arkansaw River below Ft. Lyons. I cannot tell you whether they killed my husband or not. My name is Mrs. Clara Blinn, my little boy Willie Blinn, is two years old. Do all you can for me. Write to the Peace Commissioners to make peace this fall. For our sake's do all you can and God will bless you. If you can let me hear from you. Let me know what you think about it. Write to my father and send him this. Goodbye.

Mrs. R.F. Blinn, near Antelope Hills.

I am as well as can be expected but my baby is very weak.

The letter, the last contact Clara would ever make with the rest of the world, was taken to military authorities at nearby Fort Cobb, and orders were approved that a trader could barter with Black Kettle for their release. But there was little time. Others within the U.S. military had other ambitions. Namely, Lieutenant Colonel George Armstrong Custer and the Seventh Cavalry had been called back to duty from his home in Monroe, Michigan, to embark on a mission to quell the bloody Indian raids. In a note of irony, Custer had been residing in his adopted home of Monroe, about fifteen miles north of Toledo, with his beloved wife, Libbie. He and his family had connections to northwest Ohio, as his brothers, Tom and Boston Custer, who fought alongside him in the Indian campaigns, hailed from the Wood County town of Tontogany, about eight miles from the Blinn hometown of Perrysburg.

As Clara Blinn pleaded for peace efforts to save her life and that of her son, there were in fact some peace talks underway at the time. Meetings were being held with Indian chiefs and military commanders to end the bloodshed that had become all too frequent on the plains during the year

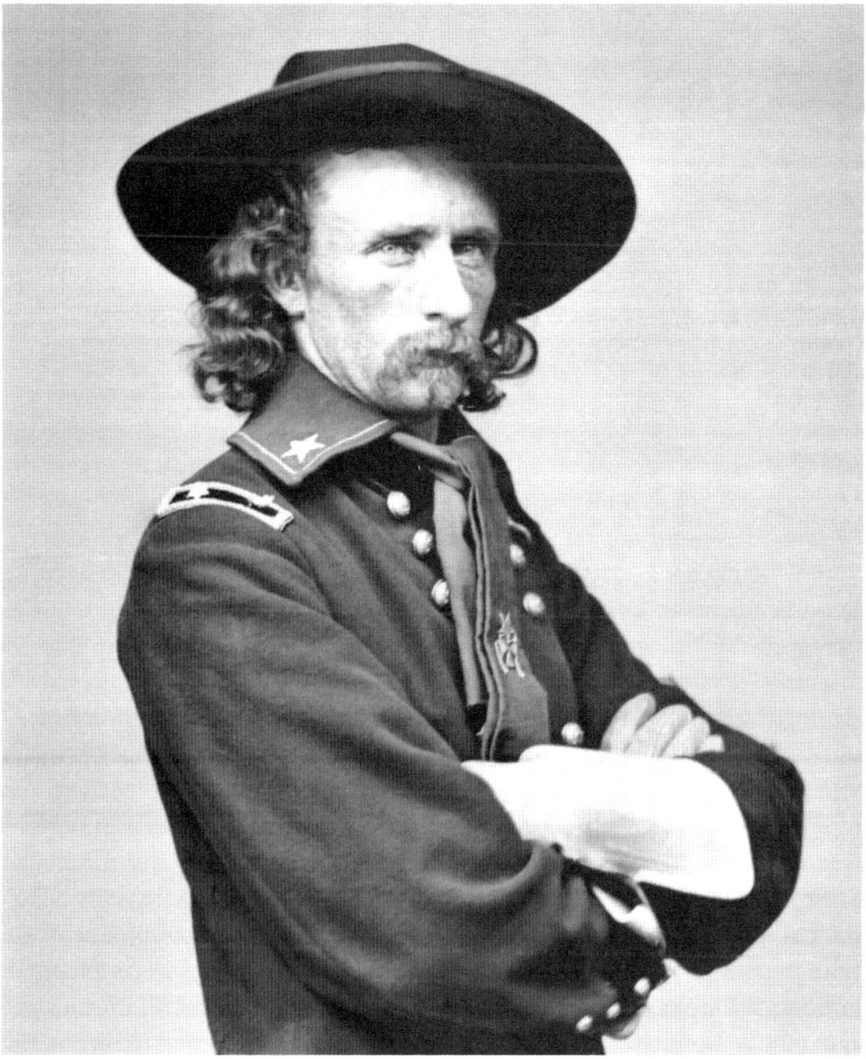

General George Armstrong Custer. *Library of Congress.*

1868. On November 20 of that year, Black Kettle traveled to Fort Cobb to plead to the commander that he and his tribe should not be punished for the actions of some of his braves who were often hard to control. He wanted to make a lasting peace and told them his encampment near the Antelope Hills along the Washita River, with 180 lodges, was a peaceful village, and he wanted it to remain so, promising not to travel north to make trouble. Black Kettle's entreaties, however, were greeted by indifference. The commander

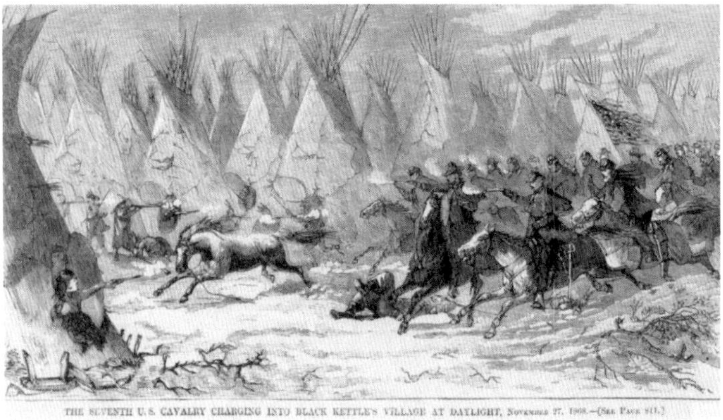

A magazine illustration of Custer's bloody raid on Washita encampment.

at Fort Cobb, Lieutenant Colonel Hazen, would only promise that if the Washita camp was attacked by the army, it would be the work of another commander and that he had no control over his superiors.

On the icy Thanksgiving morning of November 26, George Armstrong Custer and his troops were in the vicinity of the Antelope Hills in the Colorado Territory, scouring the snow-covered landscape for any sign of a winter encampment of Indian villages. He was especially interested in finding a trail that might lead them there, and as the famous "Custer luck" would have it, Major Joel Elliot, a former Toledo schoolteacher who led an advance party, had discovered signs of such a trail. It was the opportunity Custer had been waiting for. The next day, November 27, Custer's army, eight hundred strong, clad in buffalo skin clothing, looked out over the Cheyenne encampment of teepees along the Washita. Within minutes, as the day's first light cracked the horizon, Custer's musician had struck up his favorite rendition of the Irish drinking song "Garry Owen." The horses charged, and the firing commenced. The music provided an eerie backdrop to the screams of the Indians running from their teepees as the rifles barked in the hands of the soldiers on horseback. In fifteen minutes, it was mostly over. Scattered about the camp, the bodies of Indian men, women and children lay bleeding to death in the crimson-etched snow. Chief Black Kettle and his wife were among them, cut down by a barrage of bullets as they tried vainly to defend the camp. Soon after, Custer, afraid that other Indians encamped along the valley would rally with a counterattack, ordered his troops to burn the village and shoot the eight hundred Indian ponies of the Cheyenne so they could not be used by other Indians. There is no evidence that Custer knew about or ever tried to find the Perrysburg woman and her young son. In Custer's hasty retreat, he left behind his second-in-command, Major Joe

Elliot, and a detachment of eighteen troops who had pursued some fleeing Indians into an area downstream near the camp of the Kiowa. Two weeks later, Custer returned to the Washita battlefield site, and the bodies of Elliot and his men were found, dead and badly mutilated near the Kiowa camp just a few miles away from the camp of Black Kettle. It was here that soldiers also found the frozen bodies of the young Clara Blinn and her son, Willie. Clara had been shot twice in the head and her chest mutilated. There are conflicting reports as to whether she had been scalped. Army accounts say she was perhaps trying to flee, as she held in her bosom bread and meat. The young Willie had suffered hideous injuries to his head. One witness report says he had been dashed against a tree. As Perrysburg historian Judith Justus notes from her research, "There have been various scenarios written about their demise. It is a mystery."

There is no definitive or firm consensus among historians as to how they died or who killed them. Some accounts blame the Cheyenne. Others contend it was the Arapahoe. Still others offer that it was Kiowa leader Satanta himself who killed Clara and Willie. And there are even theories, and some reports, that it was Custer's soldiers who killed Clara, mistaken for an Indian during the fog of the battle. Some historians forward the theory and offer some evidence that little Willie was not killed but managed to escape the battle and lived out the balance of his life in the West.

We may never know the truth. But the sad demise of this young mother from Wood County and her son continues to occupy the center of one of the most controversial episodes of the American Indian Campaign and the exploits of Lieutenant Colonel George Custer. It is a controversy that inflamed the passions of those on both sides of the Indian debate for years. The critics of the army believed the army had been too hasty and bloodthirsty for revenge. General Philip Sheridan, however, the head of the Indian War Campaign, belittled any notion that Black Kettle was a man who was friendly and peaceful. He stated he was well satisfied with Custer's attack and made the oft-repeated and misquoted statement, "The only good Indians I ever saw were dead."

As for Clara's husband, Richard Blinn, this, too, is a sad chapter, for he did not know until months later what had actually happened to his wife and child. Following their capture in October 1868, Blinn roamed the plains areas of Colorado and the Indian Territories searching for his family in painful and tormented obsession. He kept a personal diary of his journey, which was found in the possession of a Perrysburg relative many decades later. On December 29, he wrote: "Traveled all day in the rain, walked all

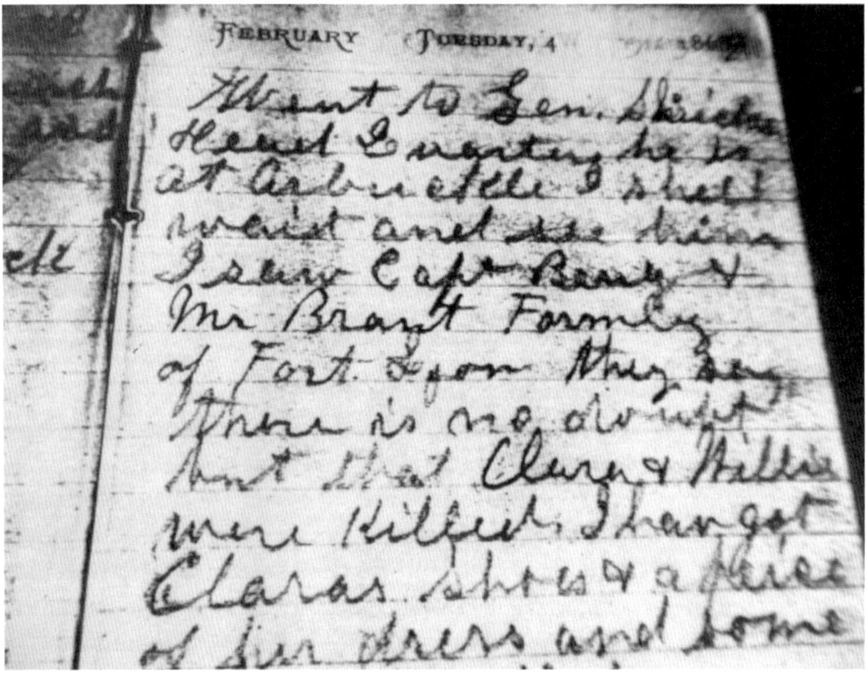

Richard Blinn kept a diary of his search for his wife, Clara, and son Willie. *Courtesy Franklin County, Kansas Historical Center.*

the time. It looks dark and gloomy and I feel the same. I would give my life for my little family, but I'm afraid I've got to go through this world alone. If I only knew where they were, I would feel better, but to live and think what they have to go through is worse than death."

On January 3, he penned:

> *Life looks darker and dreary to me. I wish I was with my wife, dead or alive. The tears will fall in spite of me when I think of the happy days that are gone to return no more. Little did I think that one year would find me alone in the world with no one but myself to take care of. Three years, it seems like yesterday that I kissed her and called her my wife for the first time. So young and yet so good. A true wife and a kind mother. I would not want a better partner to travel through this world than my darling Clara. But now she is no more, I hope she is in a better world than this.*

A few days after this diary entry, Richard Blinn would learn for certain that the bodies of his darling Clara and Willie had been found dead at Washita

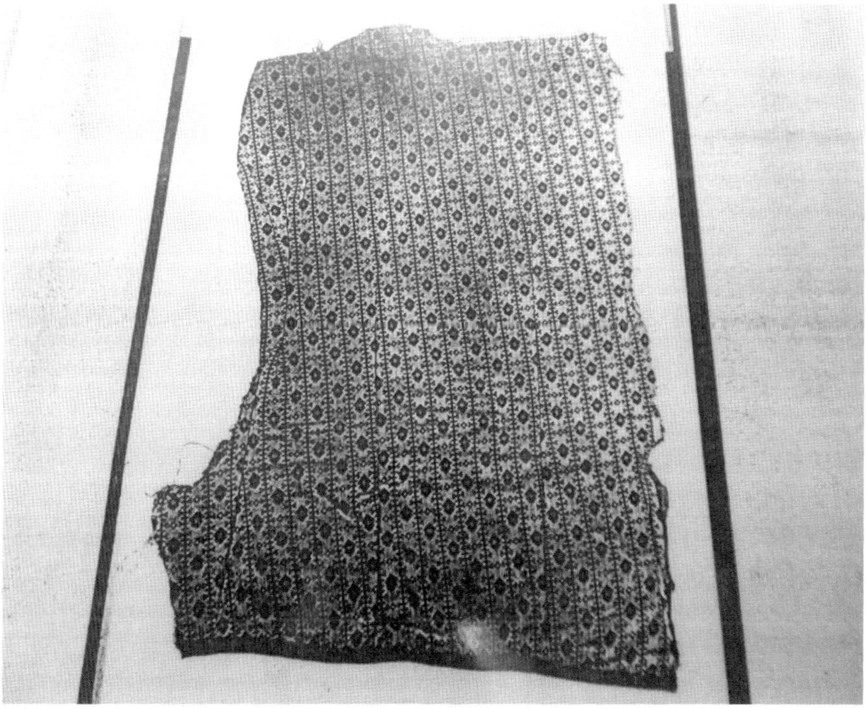

A torn remnant of Clara's dress that was recovered by cavalry soldiers and given to her husband, Richard Blinn. *Judy Justus Collection.*

River. He promised to bring them home for burial but never did. He never could. Their bodies now lie in a numbered grave at Fort Gibson, Oklahoma, after being transferred from an original grave site at Fort Arbuckle. It was from those first graves that Dick Blinn, in 1869, took two small pebbles, which he carried with him for the rest of his life. Dick would also receive a cutting from the hem of Clara's dress and a lock of Willie's hair. He would be happy to know that Clara and his son Willie are not forgotten. Her story and her courage are now remembered and honored by recent generations. There is a new memorial to her recently erected at the Washita River Battlesite in Oklahoma, while a tombstone stands at Hope Cemetery in Ottawa, Kansas, near her parents' graves. In northwest Ohio, at Fort Meigs Cemetery in Perrysburg, a memorial grave marker was placed in Clara's honor next to the grave of Richard Blinn, her loving husband, who died a few years later, in 1873, with the pain still in his heart and two small stones still in his pocket.

Chapter 4

The Summer that Changed the World

Some say radio broadcasting is dying and may not survive the new technologies of the Internet and wireless webcasting. Maybe so, maybe not. Over the decades, it's been durable and enduring. For almost every generation since its invention, it has brought us a universe of ideas, music, humor and news. Where it is headed is hard to say, but where and how it started are history—sometimes hidden. Some say the first radio station broadcast in America, maybe the world, happened in downtown Toledo in the year 1907. Surprised? Most people are, because the popular history is that those early days of radio broadcasting happened in the 1920s, when stations in Detroit and Pittsburgh were going "on the air" and claiming they were radio's first. The real "first" in wireless radio—or telephony, as it was called then—occurred in Toledo. Here's the story, as revealed by a mix of newspaper articles from the past.

This particular chapter in both the history of Toledo and radio unfolded during the heat of a rabid race by many inventors to explore this new technology called "wireless." Most of those inventors of the day were still testing how wireless could be used as a way to communicate using telegraph as the primary communication vehicle. The notion of actually transmitting a human voice and receiving it "through the air," without wires, was beyond the boundaries of even the most fertile imaginations. But great innovations require great dreams, and many of those early dreams were pursued in downtown Toledo. In a news article written by the NEA news service in 1925, Lee DeForest, considered the "father" of wireless broadcast radio, found himself in Toledo in the summer of 1907, and it was here that he made his first real breakthroughs in his quest to find a way to send voices through the air. This was a task he probably couldn't have done without the help of a northwest Ohio man and fellow believer, Frank E. Butler. Butler had been a train dispatcher and telegrapher for the New York Central Railroad in Toledo. But Butler also had a passionate interest in the possibilities of this new technology of wireless communication and conducted his own experiments to see where they might lead. He wanted to do more than just tinker; he wanted to leave his job and go to work with the renowned wireless pioneer Lee DeForest. He would write in later years in a 1924 article in *Radio Broadcast* magazine that everyone thought it was a mistake for him to leave his good-paying job with the railroad to pursue these electrical dreams with DeForest, but his passion couldn't be ignored. "The railroad position carried a large salary with abundant opportunity for advancement, while my new 'job' paid only a meager amount and offered no apparent assurance of a future. The idea of communicating through space without wires was at that time considered fantastic, an idle dream, an impossibility, a game for fools. Many thought it was a fake."

In 1904, Butler joined DeForest at the St. Louis World's Fair, where DeForest had set up a popular exhibit demonstrating to people and potential investors just how telegraph signals could be broadcast without wires. This was new abstract territory for most minds to comprehend, and many who saw the DeForest wireless telegraph machines work were still skeptical and thought it was all "fake news." Butler, however, knew better; he not only understood the technology but also grasped the enormous potential of this new science and what it could mean to the world. Butler struck up a friendship with DeForest and began working as his chief assistant. Shortly thereafter, he traveled with DeForest to Florida and Cuba to set up wireless telegraph stations for the U.S. Navy between Florida and Guantanamo Bay, Cuba.

After the navy contract was completed, Lee DeForest, who had an active ego, found himself in a legal tangle with his investors and was kicked out of his own company, American DeForest. He was left on his own to chase new horizons for this technology. Undaunted by this turn of events and a lack of funding, DeForest and Butler were determined to pursue the idea of electrically sending the human voice through air without wires. To achieve that end, DeForest had developed the so-called Audion Bulb, a crude two-element vacuum tube of sorts that allowed him to detect or amplify a radio signal. Butler and DeForest then built two crudely designed sending and receiving units and in July 1907 took them to Put-in-Bay at South Bass Island on Lake Erie to an annual yacht race. This race would become their first real test. DeForest placed the transmitter on the seventy-five-foot yacht *Thelma*, renamed the *Electra* for the race, and set up the receiving unit on shore near what is now the Jet Express dock. Frank Butler later recalled that because the yacht had a mahogany hull, he and DeForest snuck onto the boat and nailed two sheets of copper to its sides to help give it a better ground system when the copper was submerged in water. It worked. As the race progressed, DeForest was able to send to Butler, who was back on shore, voice accounts of the race as it was taking place, thus making the first "ship to shore" radio voice transmission in the world. News of this broadcast "first" was greeted with much doubt and indifference by the media and, for that matter, the rest of the world, who perhaps thought this was just exaggeration and fakery.

Butler and DeForest, however, were convinced that success of wireless voice communication was now at hand. Without any income, the two men needed a place to do their experiments. Butler convinced the inventor DeForest that they should go to Toledo, where Butler's in-laws would give them a roof over their heads and a place to live and eat. Butler had already rented space from the Spitzer family, securing the roof of the Nicholas Building in downtown Toledo so they would have a place to experiment and continue their work. The race to radio's future was running at full speed high above Toledo's downtown streets as DeForest and Butler designed and built even more radio sets in that summer of 1907. They set up laboratories in both the Nicholas and Ohio Buildings downtown, often broadcasting music from an old phonograph when they weren't talking between the two buildings. In one innovative milestone, noted in the *Toledo News Bee* in August 1907, the two men also achieved the first "phone patch" communication with their system, as DeForest talked with Butler's mother-in-law, Julia Manning, from their home at 818 Collingwood. In a phone call between the Old West End home and the Ohio Building, Butler held up the phone receiver to the microphone so Julia could talk with Lee DeForest at the Nicholas Building via the radio signal. A small achievement with big significance.

As DeForest and Butler continued showing the world what they could do, success and recognition would follow. In a 1925 interview with Butler, who was then working as a sporting goods and radio manager for a store in Toledo, he said that after the Toledo experiments, Lee DeForest got a large order for forty wireless radio sets for the U.S. Navy to be used in the fleet of Admiral Bob Evans for a round-the-world cruise of naval vessels so they could be connected with voice communication. There would be many more orders and new breakthrough and even more recognition for DeForest. The rest, as they say, is history. DeForest would go on to become known as the "Father of Radio," while Butler would eventually live out his life in Toledo in relative obscurity. He did form the American Wireless Institute and wrote about his years with DeForest, which he treasured for the rest of his life.

> *Surely, the most enthusiastic radio fan cannot realize the exceptional thrill which is now mine as I listen-in on my radio receiver and compare its wondrous achievements to those of the struggling, experimental days when I assisted Dr. De Forest in his elementary pioneer work; in the building of his first few "Audion bulbs," and shared with him the marvel of listening-in for the first time to a wireless telephone.*

Radio would, of course, have a profound effect on the world. It still does. It was the "Internet" of our grandparents' age and a miracle of communication that would change every facet of life and how we perceive it. It brought the voice of the world to our living rooms and to our minds.

More than a century has passed since the summer of 1907 when radio history was made in Toledo. The Nicholas and Ohio Buildings still stand; Lee DeForest remains a giant in radio history; a special sign commemorates the first "ship to shore broadcast" at Put-in-Bay; and Frank E. Butler, who died in January 1948 at the age of seventy-one, is remembered only by a few as the young man who dared to live a dream that changed the world.

Chapter 5

Toledo's Biggest Robbery

In the early morning darkness of February 17, 1921, young Joseph Hughes of North Toledo was just doing his job, driving a truck from Union Station, where he had just picked up a shipment of mail that had come in from the East on the New York Central and another load that came up from Cincinnati on the Baltimore & Ohio (B&O). He was taking the sacks of mail to the new main post office on Fourteenth Street between Madison and Jefferson Avenues. He didn't notice that behind him, furtively following, was a big black Studebaker sedan—one that had been stolen just two nights before and was bearing stolen plates that had been stripped off a car in the downtown area on Wednesday. Inside was a gang of men with guns. What started as a typical and routine Thursday morning was about to be the biggest day of Hughes's young life. As he wheeled the mail truck from Jefferson Avenue onto Fourteenth Street to park in the portico to make the delivery, it was then he may have noticed the black sedan coming in right behind him. As Joe Hughes pulled in and got out to help a fellow mail clerk remove the bags from the truck, two men with revolvers came up behind them and began barking orders: "C'mon, men, up with them, it's a stick-up!" The two postal workers put their hands up in the air, and one of the gunmen told them to lie facedown on the loading dock. They did as they were told. Then more men jumped out of the bandits' car, slipped into the back of the mail truck and started grabbing sacks of mail, and in a bucket brigade fashion, they began transferring them to their car. There were eleven sacks in all, and within minutes, the bandits had what they had come for. One of the gang called, "All aboard!" and the rest of the robbers jumped on the car, some still clinging to the running boards as they sped off into the darkness of Toledo's streets. The whole affair took about three minutes. No shots were fired, but it was an unnerving experience for some of the workers who weren't sure if they would survive. Just one month before this robbery, two railroad detectives in Toledo were shot dead during a robbery as they left Union Station with $10,000 in payroll cash. While no one was shot or killed in this stick-up, it was no less dramatic, for this would prove to be far more than a simple robbery.

Within a couple of days, Toledo police determined that this crime was likely the work of the Urbaytis Gang, led by two brothers, Joe and Frank Urbaytis, who had been in and out of trouble in the past, including bank robberies and a recent payroll robbery. Even after seventeen arrests, Joe Urbaytis was only convicted twice and never held behind bars for long.

In the meantime, federal authorities were trying to ascertain the value of the loot taken. It was a mix of cash, bonds, stocks and other securities. Early estimates put the take at no less than $1 million, maybe more. In today's dollars, that would be worth about $12 million, making it the biggest heist in Toledo history and perhaps U.S. history.

The Toledo Police Museum still has the file from the robbery, and the faded contents help fill in the blanks of the investigation that was carried out by Toledo police and federal officials as they tried to figure out just who had pulled off this stunning caper and how. The file tells a compelling story of how TPD officers worked for days to find Joe Urbaytis, whom they had suspected from the start of the case. They had also suspected he might flee to Chicago along with his familiar compatriots, George Rogers, Charles "Split Lip" Schultz and Joe Culbert. On the evening of February 22, 1921, police and railway detectives, working from a tip, found Urbaytis and some of those gang members on board the Toledo-to-Chicago train near Elkhart, Indiana. A woman, thought to be Joe's sister Wanda, managed to elude police. She was carrying the suitcase that contained much of the loot from the robbery.

By the time the plot's mastermind, Joe Urbaytis, was formally charged a week after the heist, police had also picked up several other reputed suspected members, including Schultz and several other suspected gang members. By May 1921, the list of people involved in one way or another grew to almost humorous levels as Toledo police identified more than thirty people who were thought to have knowledge or in some way have participated. One of them was Polish-speaking Father Anthony Goreck, a Chicago-area priest who was said to be friendly with Joe's sister Wanda when he was a priest at

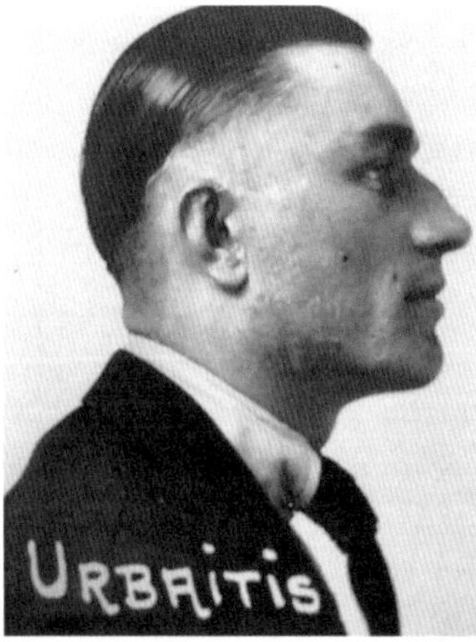

Left: Postal robber Joe Urbaytis, mugshot profile. *Courtesy Toledo Police Museum.*

Below: Newspaper articles about the 1921 postal robbery. *Courtesy Toledo Police Museum.*

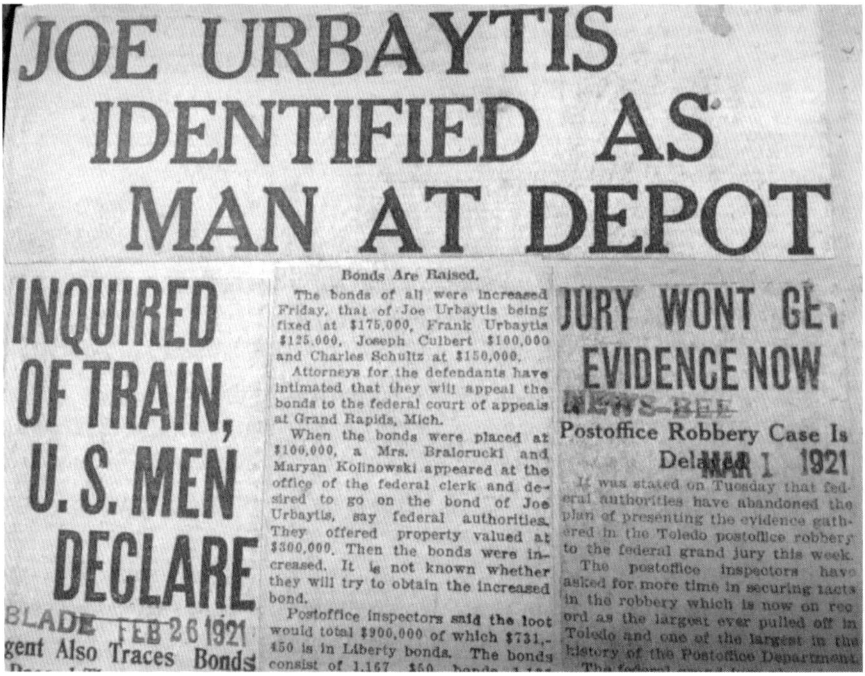

JOE URBAYTIS IDENTIFIED AS MAN AT DEPOT

INQUIRED OF TRAIN, U.S. MEN DECLARE

BLADE FEB 26 1921

gent Also Traces Bonds

Bonds Are Raised.

The bonds of all were increased Friday, that of Joe Urbaytis being fixed at $175,000, Frank Urbaytis $125,000, Joseph Culbert $100,000 and Charles Schultz at $150,000.

Attorneys for the defendants have intimated that they will appeal the bonds to the federal court of appeals at Grand Rapids, Mich.

When the bonds were placed at $100,000, a Mrs. Bralorucki and Maryan Kolinowski appeared at the office of the federal clerk and desired to go on the bond of Joe Urbaytis, say federal authorities. They offered property valued at $300,000. Then the bonds were increased. It is not known whether they will try to obtain the increased bond.

Postoffice inspectors said the loot would total $900,000 of which $731,450 is in Liberty bonds. The bonds consist of 1,167 $50 ...

JURY WONT GE[T] EVIDENCE NOW

NEWS-BEE

Postoffice Robbery Case Is Delayed

MAR 1 1921

It was stated on Tuesday that federal authorities have abandoned the plan of presenting the evidence gathered in the Toledo postoffice robbery to the federal grand jury this week.

The postoffice inspectors have asked for more time in securing facts in the robbery which is now on record as the largest ever pulled off in Toledo and one of the largest in the history of the Postoffice Department.

Toledo's St. Hedwigs. The priest had been given about $80,000 in Liberty Bonds for his church in Chicago. Others involved included those who helped in the getaway and others who helped launder the loot. It was a tangled web of various characters and plot twists. When the trial opened in Toledo federal court in June, the atmosphere was circus-like, with a crowd of defendants, attorneys, spectators and press jamming the courthouse. The scene outside the courthouse steps was a sea of straw boater hats as hundreds of men and women struggled to get inside. Once they made it, every available space in the courtroom was filled with the bodies of the curious, who even sat on the floor and on file cabinets to get a seat for what was probably the "best show in town." The only men absent from the spectacle were two of the accused armed bandits who were at the scene of the robbery. James Colson and Eddie O'Brien remained on the run. But as the trial opened, federal prosecutors felt confident they had the narrative of the crime figured out. With the confessions of several defendants in hand, they had managed to piece together the whole story. Especially important was the vital information given to them from accused bandit George Rogers, who openly laid bare to the detectives the plot, the planning and the players involved.

By the end of June, the complex and intense trial was over. Eleven people were convicted of conspiracy and two were acquitted, while many others had either confessed earlier or had charges dropped, including Joe's brother Frank Urbaytis. Facing twelve years in prison and a $10,000 fine for these initial convictions of conspiracy was the ringleader, Joe Urbaytis, along with George Rogers and Charles Schultz. They were not, however, free of even more charges, as they still faced an October trial for the robbery itself. The trio had other plans. On Labor Day weekend, September 5, they managed to violently overpower the guards, steal their guns and slip through the thick walls of the Lucas County Jail to freedom.

The trio proved to be elusive, but the search to find them was unrelenting, as Police Chief Herbert assigned more than forty officers to the hunt. As the officers believed they may have just "planted" themselves in a Toledo hiding spot for a while, many known brothels or places of low repute or criminal activity were scoured but turned up nothing. Rumors and tips flooded the police station, and there were theories that the men had escaped to Canada or Mexico. There was even speculation that the guards may not have tried hard enough to stop the escape, and two deputies who were overpowered were later fired for negligence.

A week later, Charles "Split Lip" Schultz was found hiding in the attic of a home on Crissey Road, where he had forced the resident woman and her husband to let him hole up. He went back to trial, was found guilty on more counts and was then sent to Leavenworth prison for forty years. George Rogers lasted a few months on the lam but was eventually nabbed living in a park in Chicago. Four days later, in Toledo, he was sentenced to sixty-seven years at Leavenworth. But still enjoying his freedom was the mastermind, Joe Urbaytis, who managed to give police the slip for the next

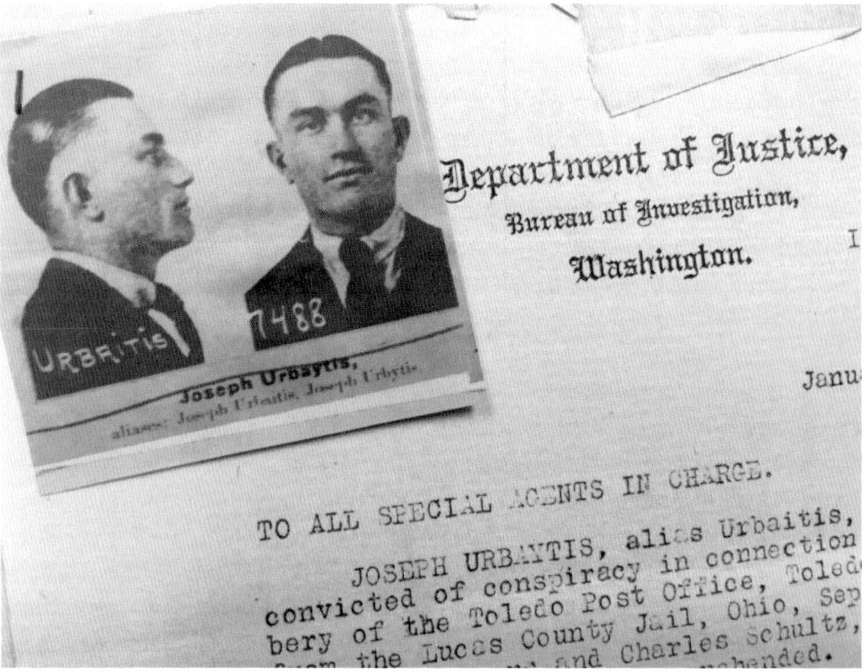

Joe Urbaytis, robber and escape artist, was considered a top criminal by the FBI. *Courtesy Toledo Police Museum.*

three years. Then, because trouble usually follows the troubled, Urbaytis turned up again in 1924, in Columbus, Ohio, where he was involved in a dramatic gun battle with police and was shot. Seriously wounded, he lay in a Columbus hospital and allowed reporters in for bedside interviews and photos. He reveled in his notoriety as a popular public enemy. Once he recovered, Urbaytis was sent back to Toledo under heavy guard, where he was convicted of his additional robbery and escape charges. With a sixty-year sentence, Joe was shipped off to a federal prison in Atlanta. True to his character, he attempted to bust out of the penitentiary—not once, but twice. His second escape attempt almost succeeded in 1928, but not quite. His freedom was short-lived, and he surrendered. After that dash for freedom, prison officials decided Joe Urbaytis was too dangerous to be left alone in the general population. Solitary confinement and isolation became routine for the Toledo postal robber, as he was considered a hardcore troublemaker. His truculent and rebellious swagger earned him a new cell at Leavenworth prison in Kansas. In 1934, still noncompliant, he was shipped off to "the Rock": the notorious escape-proof Alcatraz Prison in San Francisco Bay.

Some men tried to escape over the years. None was successful, unless death is considered freedom.

The story could have ended there, and Urbaytis might have died behind the cold bars of those prison walls and perhaps in obscurity, but once again, Joe managed to escape. This time it was not by criminal means but by virtue of a shortened sentence and a second chance at freedom. In 1943, Urbaytis was released and came home to Toledo. Not one to assume a low profile, Joe thumbed his nose at authorities in the area and flaunted his new freedom by opening an unlicensed nightclub and gambling house on Woodville Road. It was just outside the Toledo city limits in Oregon Township, not far from the railroad overpass. It was called the Bon-Aire Supper Club, and by all accounts, Joe was making money but apparently making enemies as well. In the early morning hours of November 5, 1946, Joe's luck ran out. Someone came to the back door and met Joe there. Two gunshots were heard. The bullets tore through Joe's body—one in the lungs, one in the heart. The gunman fled while Urbaytis, clinging to life, was dying. A worker in the club ran to his side to ask if he knew who shot him. If Joe knew, he would not say. It was believed by the police that he did know, but true to the "code," he wouldn't give up the truth. This time, Joe did not escape. Death claimed him minutes later. His life of crime was over. Toledo police chief Ray Allen even wrote a letter to FBI chief J. Edgar Hoover letting him know that Urbaytis had been shot and killed and the FBI could close the books on him for good.

But not quite.

The story of who killed Toledo's most famous robber and why is still unsettled history. Strange circumstances always surrounded the murder. The murder weapon was a gun that had belonged to the Toledo police chief of detectives, George Timiney, and which he had reported stolen from his car about six months before. Some witnesses claimed that Joe Urbaytis himself had possession of the gun just before the murder. The gun was not found at the scene of the crime but mysteriously several days later on the lawn of Joe's mother's house on Lagrange Street. The man who was collared for the killing was a well-known small-time gangster by the name of Frankie Burns. He was sixty-nine years old, and the evidence against him was weak, but he was charged with first-degree murder. Strangely, in a highly questioned development, the judge held a hastily called after-hours court session and allowed Burns to plea down to a manslaughter charge, thus getting about a year in prison. The public was not easy with this turn of events and wanted to know what had happened. What was the motive? There were accusations that the judicial proceedings were too opaque and smacked of secrecy. The

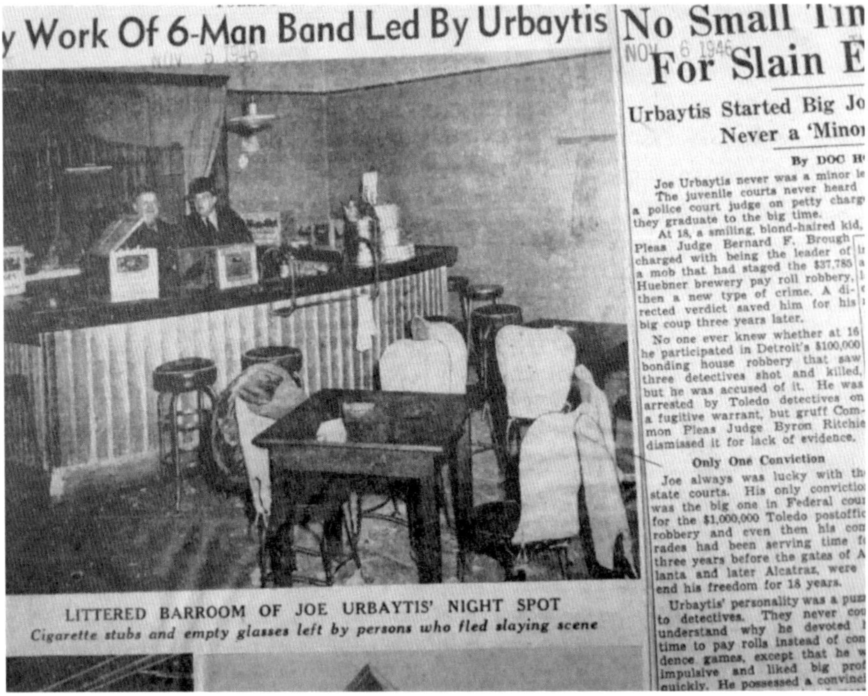

y Work Of 6-Man Band Led By Urbaytis

NOV 6 1946

LITTERED BARROOM OF JOE URBAYTIS' NIGHT SPOT

Cigarette stubs and empty glasses left by persons who fled slaying scene

No Small Tin
For Slain E

Urbaytis Started Big Jo
Never a 'Mino

By DOC H

Joe Urbaytis never was a minor le
The juvenile courts never heard
a police court judge on petty charg
they graduate to the big time.
At 18, a smiling, blond-haired kid,
Pleas Judge Bernard F. Brough
charged with being the leader of
a mob that had staged the $37,785
Huebner brewery pay roll robbery,
then a new type of crime. A di-
rected verdict saved him for his
big coup three years later.

No one ever knew whether at 16
he participated in Detroit's $100,000
bonding house robbery that saw
three detectives shot and killed,
but he was accused of it. He was
arrested by Toledo detectives on
a fugitive warrant, but gruff Com-
mon Pleas Judge Byron Ritchie
dismissed it for lack of evidence.

Only One Conviction

Joe always was lucky with th
state courts. His only convictio
was the big one in Federal cou
for the $1,000,000 Toledo postoffic
robbery and even then his com
rades had been serving time f
three years before the gates of A
lanta and later Alcatraz, were
end his freedom for 18 years.

Urbaytis' personality was a puz
to detectives. They never co
understand why he devoted
time to pay rolls instead of con
dence games, except that he w
impulsive and liked big pro
quickly. He possessed a convinc

Newswire photo showing murder scene inside Bon Aire Supper Club. *Toledo Police Museum.*

public sensed something amiss. Maybe so. After Burns was convicted, he quickly recanted, claiming he had been set up and framed and had nothing to do with the murder of Urbaytis. Upon his release from prison, a few years later, he also would be murdered.

It may be nearly a century since Joe Urbaytis pulled off Toledo's biggest heist, and everyone involved has long since been buried, but for crime historians, many questions have yet to be answered; maybe they never will. It's almost as if Joe Urbaytis escaped again, and his whole story still hasn't surrendered to the truth.

Chapter 6

The Famous Mail Train Dog Whose Travels Ended in Toledo

Some historical events Toledo can lay claim to and be proud of; others—not so much. The story of Owney the famous postal dog is one that goes into Toledo's "we'd-rather-not-talk-about-it" file. But Toledo in the past few years has had to confront a century-old embarrassment.

If you don't know the story of Owney, it all started back in roughly 1888 when this scruffy Irish-Scottish terrier mongrel took up residence in the Albany, New York post office. It is recounted that Owney loved the scent of the mail bags and began riding the mail wagons, and then one day, he hopped onto a rail car, nestled himself atop the mail sacks and went to sleep. Thus began his travels on the mail trains. Whether it is true remains elusive. There was one story printed that lends credence to the lore.

The 1891 article notes that the dog "is never happy unless he is in a car, surrounded with mail bags....Some of his admirers tried to get him photographed recently. They took him up to the photographer's place, but no amount of coaxing, petting and threatening could make him keep quiet. Finally his friends sent for some mail bags and threw them on the floor. The dog at once lay on top of them. The trick worked and the session was under way."

Whatever the truth may be, Owney's legacy and legend as a rail-riding canine was carved quickly by the press, eager to sell newspapers. Within a few years, Owney was hopping rides on these mail cars on a regular routine, and quite independently at that. When he turned up at different postal stations along his routes, postal employees loved it and would affix a postal

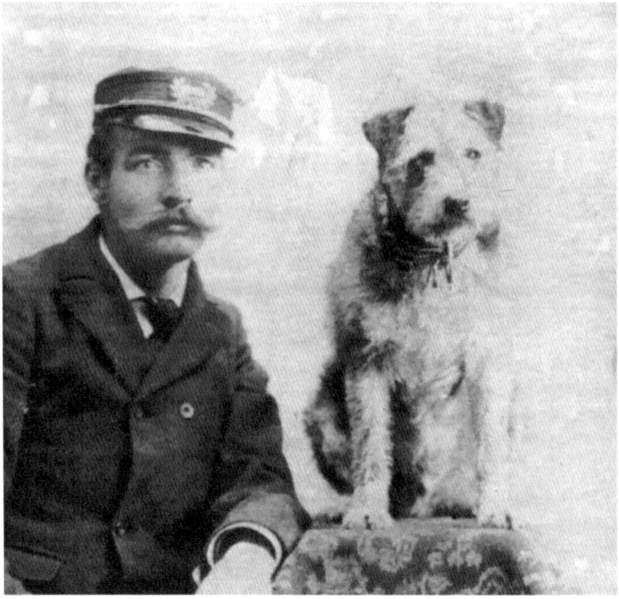

Owney posing with a postal worker. *Courtesy Smithsonian Museum.*

tag to his collar. Postmaster General John Wanamaker was one of Owney's fans. Upon hearing that the dog's collar was weighted down by his hundreds of tags, he gave Owney a harness on which to display the "trophies." The traveling terrier of the rails soon became laden with a chandelier of tags. In 1894, a writer for the *Brooklyn Daily Eagle* reported that "nearly every place he stopped Owney received an additional tag, until now he wears a big bunch. When he jogs along, they jingle like the bells on a junk wagon."

The scruffy mutt was not the best-looking dog by far and probably would not win any prizes at a dog show, but rail employees thought he might be a good luck charm since never once did a train wreck while he was on board—and rail accidents were not uncommon in that era. The postal employees loved this hairy vagabond, who was blind in one eye from a lost fight. They tried to wash him as often as they could, but Owney would often work hard to undo the grooming effort so he could return his body to a scruffy, unkempt look. It was rather amazing how this mutt who could do no tricks made such an impression. Owney was also said to be an excellent ratter and could catch rats by the score while he visited some of the postal stations. The public loved the stories about this dubious wonder dog and wanted to read more tales of the traveling terrier of the rails. Newspaper reporters and photographers were eager to oblige and often called to snap a picture of Owney when he rolled into town.

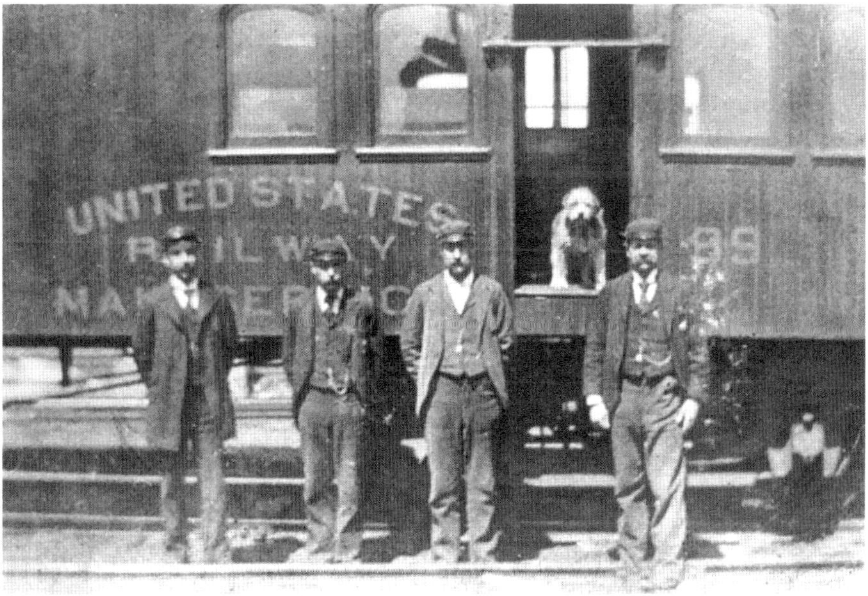

Above: Owney with postal workers posing in a rail car, circa 1890. *Courtesy Smithsonian Museum.*

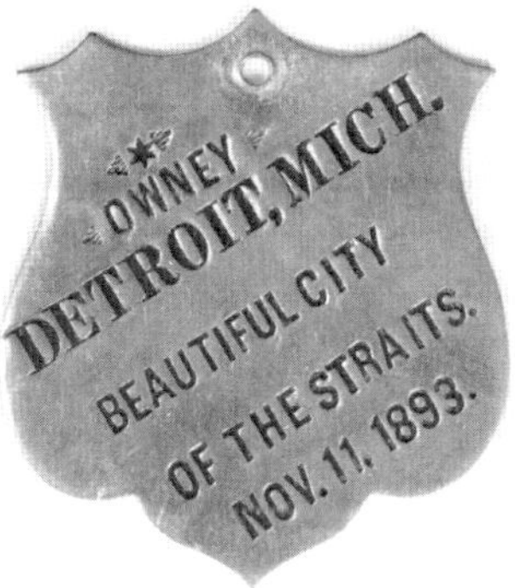

Left: One of the many postal tags issued to Owney during his travels around the United States. *Courtesy Smithsonian Museum.*

Owney's most exciting adventure that sealed his fame forever with the world was his trip around the globe—by himself. In October 1895, with only his vest of medals and tags and an introductory letter to officials of other nations, he was put on a ship to Yokohama, Japan, and then proceeded to tour parts of Asia and Europe. For almost one hundred days, he traveled alone, wagging his tail and visiting the far corners of the earth. His journey afforded him the chance to meet the emperor of China, the prince of Wales and the king of Italy. By the end of December, he was back in New York City to a jubilant waiting crowd and soon was back home in Albany. Owney was indeed a larger-than-life celebrity, and it can be argued that he was the first and biggest real "dog star" in the United States, long before there was a Lassie or a Rin Tin Tin. As more than one story noted, he "has attained more distinction in this country than the average human citizen can hope for" and has "traveled more miles than some of the wealthiest sightseers." Some of the dog's fans believed that he really had the soul of a man, perhaps an old postal clerk who had died and whose soul had taken up residence with Owney.

As revered as he was, the affection was not universal. Not everyone loved Owney. In April 1897, the Chicago postmaster was disgusted by Owney's presence on the rail cars and postal stations, calling him a mongrel cur who was nothing more than a nuisance to employees and saying that he should be banned from the rails. Those rancorous remarks were widely reported at the time and were shared by others of the same mind-set who were not enamored with animals. This included the postmaster at Toledo, who also found Owney to be a mean-spirited nuisance.

Postal Museum historians say that by May 1897, Owney was in poor health, and it was decided to retire him from the rails; thus, he went to live with a postal employee in St. Louis. Newspaper accounts headlined "Owney Is Not Dead" say he went to live with a man by the name of J.H. Melvin during his remaining years. The same story also discounted a report from Cleveland that the postal pooch had been shot and killed by a policeman in that city. It wasn't true, as the article explained that the dog shot by the policeman in Cleveland was just an "ordinary mangy cur" and not the famous Owney. But somehow, by some twist of fate, little more than a month later, on June 11, 1897, Owney would be shot to death. In Toledo.

There are several varying accounts of what took place, but according to the *Chicago Tribune*, when Owney—who somehow found his way back on the trains—arrived at Toledo's Union Station that night, a postal clerk called a newspaper reporter and photographer to get some pictures and a story. The clerk had chained Owney up to a post to keep him there while awaiting the arrival of the photographer. One account says that Owney detested being tied up or restrained and started protesting loudly, and when a postal clerk by the name of Blankhertz tried to get him to quiet down, Owney bit him on the hand. That action prompted the Toledo postmaster, Rudolph Brand, to ask U.S. marshal Shannan to come to the scene, but Owney rushed him and tore his trousers. Postmaster Brand called the chief of police and demanded that Owney be killed. Different newspapers have differing angles of this, but the *Chicago Tribune* says a police officer named Fred Free shot and killed Owney while he was still chained to the post. The *Chicago Tribune* called it

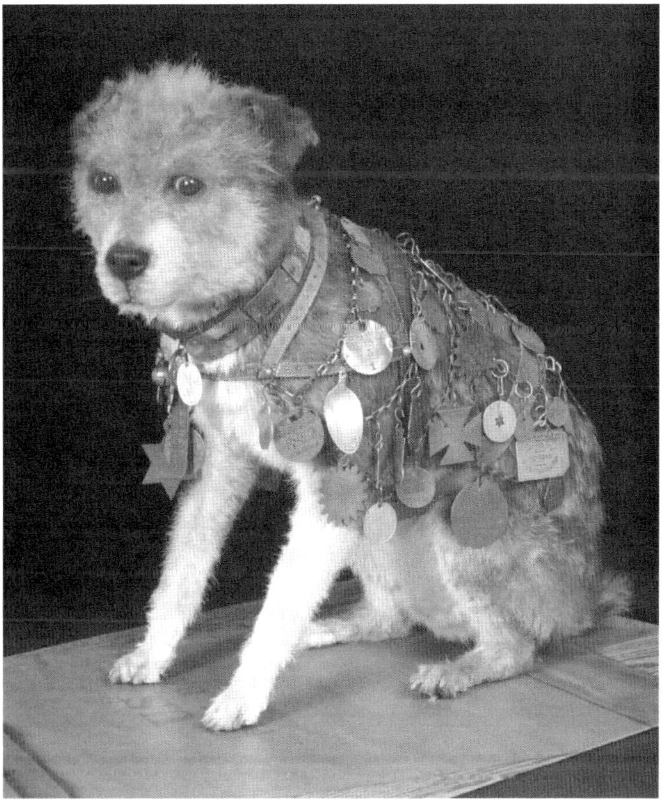

Right: Owney's remains were preserved by taxidermists in Toledo after being shot by Toledo police. He is on display at the Smithsonian Postal Museum. *Courtesy Smithsonian Museum.*

Below: Owney was recently memorialized with his own postage stamp. *Courtesy U.S. Postal Service.*

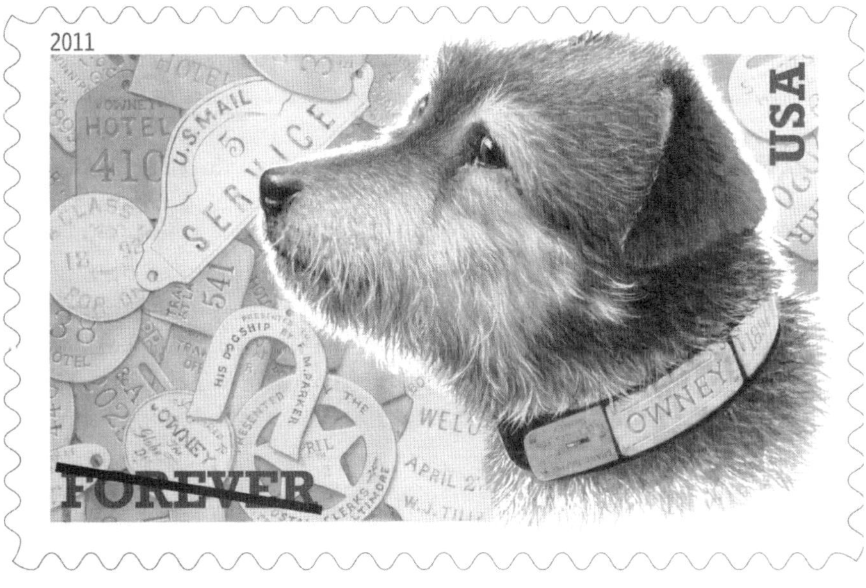

an "execution," while other newspaper accounts (perhaps engaging some damage control) said Owney had been running loose and "had gone mad" when he was shot.

One newspaper account claims Owney was not killed immediately after the biting incident but his execution was delayed until the next day, owing to the fact that the first policeman who was ordered to shoot the globe-trotting pooch refused to do so. As a result, Postmaster Brand had Owney chained to a post until the next day, when he was taken away and shot by a patrolman named Smith. "Shortly after 4 o'clock yesterday, Patrolman Smith took the dog to an alley behind the police station and with a shot put an end to the career of the famous pup."

Call it the blur of history or the fog of time, or conspiracy among the guilty, but we may never know exactly what happened in Toledo or why the world's most famous dog met his fate that day.

When word surfaced in Toledo that the famous mail pooch's stamp had been canceled, mail clerks throughout the city raised funds to have the cinnamon-colored terrier's skin stuffed and preserved. The taxidermy took place in Toledo, and the effigy of the little seventeen-year-old dog was eventually given to the Post Office Department's headquarters in Washington, D.C. It remained there, on display, with a few trips to world's fairs and expositions. Then, in 1911, Owney was transferred to the Smithsonian Institute in Washington, where he has been on display in a glass case ever since.

In recent years, Owney's amazing story has found resonance with a new generation of children and admirers. In 2011, Owney was given the honor of his own postage stamp. He also had his mounted remains cleaned and restored and put on a more prominent display at the Postal Museum at the Smithsonian. As more people discover this American story, they have been inspired to write books about his travels, create travel toys in his likeness and produce songs and plays about him.

Little did those who played a role in Owney's tragic demise in Toledo ever imagine in those days just how famous the little guy would become in the future. Or maybe they did? As emotions ran high in the country about the killing of Owney, it was noted by a *Blade* reporter at the time that Owney's tragic death would "bring down the wrath of the heavens" upon the heads of those involved.

We can't be sure if such wrath ever came to visit, but Owney did. In the 1930s, his glass-encased stuffed remains were returned to Toledo for a visit during a postal clerks' convention.

CHAPTER 7

THE BEAUTIFUL JUNE MACCLOY

Toledo's Forgotten Star

When June Mary MacCloy passed away in 2005, few in Toledo probably knew it—or probably knew her or remembered her. There was a small obit printed in the *Blade* (ten days later) and one line referencing her early life in Toledo. Perhaps this is understandable, since it had been over sixty years since her star in the Hollywood constellation blipped out and went dark. Yes, June MacCloy was a Toledo girl, the proverbial hometown girl who made good. For this beautiful young woman, it was both in the footlights of Broadway and under the bright lights of Hollywood. She was a statuesque blond actress who epitomized the glamour era of Hollywood and probably could have and should have made an even bigger name for herself. The Scott High School graduate was also blessed (or cursed, some would say) with an unusual singing voice—so deep and rich and husky that it was perceived by some as very manly, albeit still very good. Still, there were critics who believed that her voice was a liability, and there were always rumors that she was a lesbian, which during that era of more provincial sexual mores may have also affected her career.

June MacCloy's professional career on stage and screen lasted for about twenty-two years, starting in 1928 in New York and ending with a final movie appearance in 1940 in the rollicking Marx Brothers' comedy *Go West*. Cast in the role of the sexy Lulubelle, a saloonkeeper and dance hall girl, this Toledo girl was said by the critics to be "a worthy match" for the inimitable talents of Groucho Marx, who greets her in one scene saying, "Lulubelle! I didn't recognize you standing up." To which she replies, with hands on her

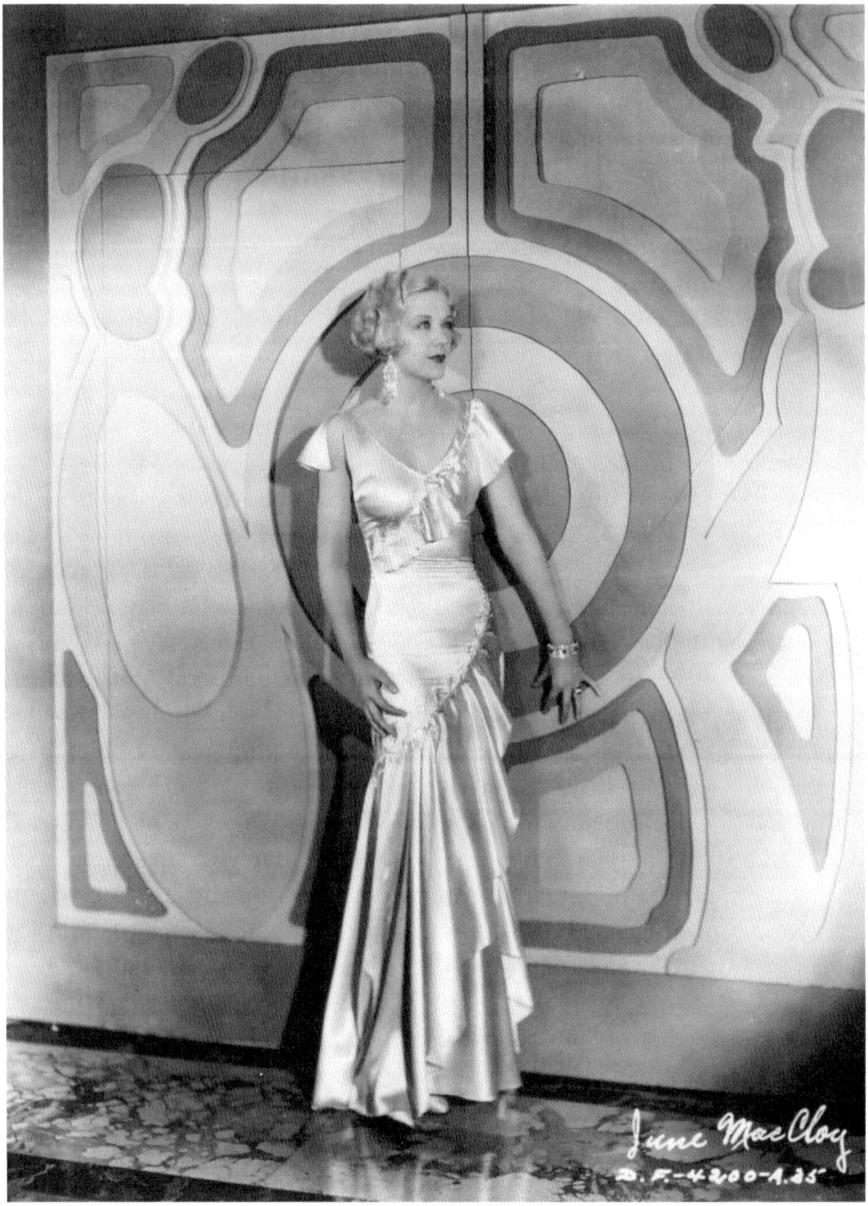

The pretty June MacCloy posing for a publicity still from the movie *Reaching for the Moon*. *Peter Mintun Collection.*

hips, "Vamoosh, you goose." She then croons the song "You Can't Argue with Love." Lulubelle next sits on Groucho's knee, with a knowing wink, and concludes the song as he clings to her while they stand on a small table.

June Mary MacCloy's story began just north of the Indiana state line in Sturgis, Michigan, where she was born on June 2, 1909. Her family, however, moved to Toledo when she was still a girl, as her father, Louis, worked in one of Toledo's many auto plants. Their first home was said to be in the 1400 block of Franklin Avenue. It was here that she was raised and matured into a tall and good-looking girl who could turn heads with her striking beauty and a radiant smile of pearly teeth. By the time she was in her mid-teens, she was starting to perform in plays and musicals in schools and amateur productions in Toledo. She got the bug for theater and wanted to pursue such a career. Her mother was wary, but okay with the idea, and allowed June to leave her humble home for the bright lights of Broadway and the Big Apple. It didn't take long before the striking young willowy blonde found work and joined Earl Carroll's *Vanities* on Broadway in 1928; however, the show was not a paragon of modesty, and she was convinced to leave the revue after complaints from her mother that her costume was too revealing. MacCloy recalled later that the outfit she wore was "basically strings of cotton candy and Mother thought one of the rich guys in the audience would rape me or something. Although that kind of thing did happen, I always managed to stay out of harm's way."

MacCloy's masculine baritone voice led her next to work as a male impersonator, mimicking the style of Broadway star Harry Richman with the song "I'm on the Crest of a Wave" while playing in George White's long-running Broadway revue *Scandals*. She performed the song 230 times at the Apollo Theater in a production that launched the careers of many notables of the era.

It was written in her obit by longtime friend Peter Mintun that she continued working in vaudeville during the 1920s and '30s and had the chance to work with the famed director Vincent Minnelli (husband of Judy Garland and father of Liza Minelli), whom MacCloy recalled as a sadistic "nut" and a perfectionist with a "sexual craving for his own kind."

Her film career began in 1931, when MacCloy was "lent out" to Paramount Pictures to make her first feature film, *Reaching for the Moon*, with Douglas Fairbanks Sr., Bebe Daniels and a very young Bing Crosby. On her way from New York to Hollywood to begin production, the Scott High School graduate made a stop in Toledo on the train to visit family and talk with reporters.

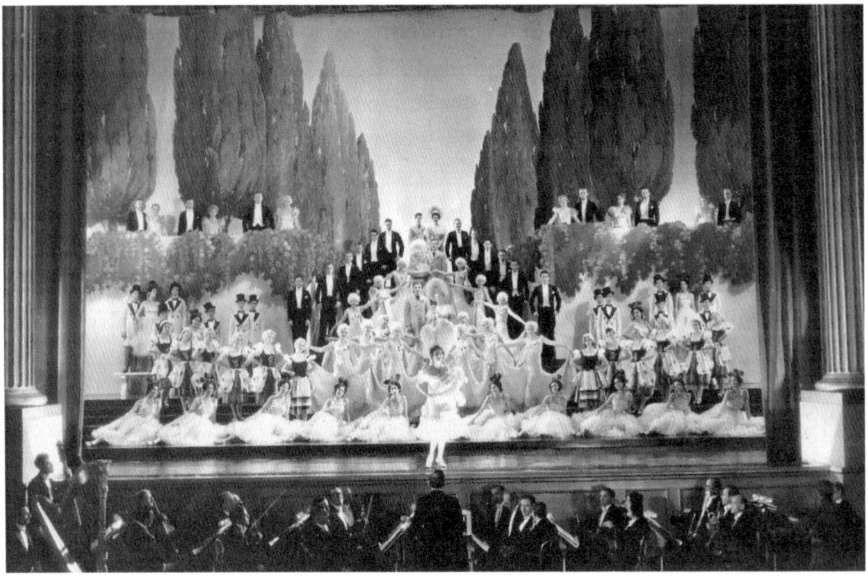

June MacCloy in chorus for the movie *Reaching for the Moon*.

The September 18, 1930 *Toledo News Bee* carried a story and picture of the young and promising hometown girl who had just landed a $12,000 contract with Paramount to begin her career in the motion picture industry. The *News Bee* wrote that MacCloy was "the first Toledo woman to ever do a talking motion picture." It was also noted by Paramount that a $12,000 contract was no small beans, saying, "Not since the rise of Jeanette MacDonald has a player so comparatively little-known as Miss MacCloy been signed by Paramount for such a figure."

She was received in Hollywood warmly and adapted quickly to the creative climate of the growing film colony. Her performance in her film debut earned some good reviews, especially for her rendition of Irving Berlin's "When the Folks High Up Do the Mean Down Low." The *Los Angeles Times* wrote, "With a little encouragement, she could have stolen the show."

After her silver screen debut in *Reaching for the Moon*, she would go on to some success and notice in Ring Lardner and George Kaufman's *June Moon* with Frances Dee and Jack Oakie. This movie could have been her big break, but the picture did not live up to its billing, and MacCloy's career never seemed to get the traction it needed to develop its full potential. She did appear in nine film shorts in the 1930s, including *Laugh It Off* by Paramount, *The Gay Girls*, *June First* and *Only Men Wanted*. The famous

Roscoe "Fatty" Arbuckle directed several of the films. "Fatty Arbuckle was a peach of a guy," MacCloy later said. Most of June MacCloy's films are still available for viewing on movie websites, including the Marx Brothers classic *Go West*, in which Groucho Marx uttered the famous pick-up line to MacCloy, "Let's go somewhere we can be alone. Oh, there doesn't seem to be anyone on this couch."

Groucho was impressed with MacCloy's talent and wanted her to star with him in other movies, but June said she wanted to be a serious actress and didn't think Marx Brothers comedies was where she wanted her career to go. Sadly, her career never went anywhere after *Go West*. It was her last film.

For a period of time in the 1930s after finding fame in Hollywood, she returned to the New York stage. On Broadway, in 1932, she appeared with Lupe Velez, Bert Lahr, Buddy Rogers and June Knight in *Hot-Cha*, Florenz Ziegfeld's last production. Her featured song was "Little Old New York."

When *Hot-Cha* closed after 119 performances, MacCloy took her act on the cruise ship SS *Transylvania* and then spent the rest of the decade performing in Chicago, New York and San Francisco clubs and theaters with the leading orchestras of that era and playing the best nightclubs.

Her son Newton says she also performed for special events outside Hollywood, for many famous faces from the 1930s, including Chicago gangster Lucky Luciano and others. He recalls, "All of them she found perfect gentlemen and I suspect appreciated their innate protectiveness of a lady performer who sang in the night spots where they felt temporarily 'safe' enough to kick back for an evening." Miss MacCloy also performed at the Hotel Mark Hopkins in San Francisco and told friend Peter Mintun during an interview that "the biggest compliment was when the dancers stopped in front of the orchestra when I started to sing."

During her years in the glare of Hollywood, the stunning MacCloy was a favorite of the gossip columnists and show biz tabloids, as her looks symbolized the Golden Age of Hollywood. She was so good looking that there were always plenty of stories about her army of admirers. She said in later interviews that many men at that time proposed marriage, using the lure of money and diamonds. One of those men was Jimmy Whiting, a multimillionaire playboy type in Hollywood who tried putting a ring on MacCloy's finger. There was little doubt that he had plenty of money to employ in his campaign for wedlock, and on one occasion, he even arranged a flight in a plane filled with rose petals. But it was not to be. Whiting's chief rival for MacCloy's heart turned out to be a Toledo boy by the name of

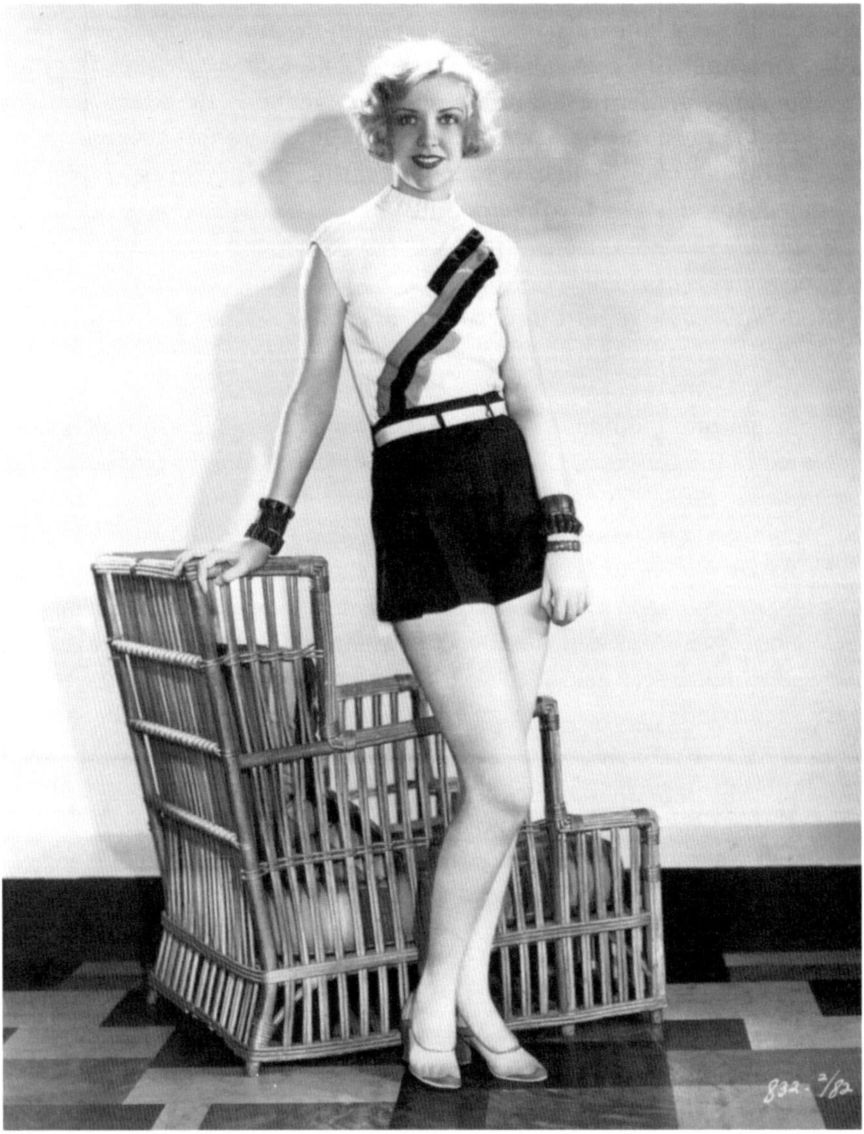

June MacCloy's legs were as famous as her low-contralto voice. *Peter Mintun Collection.*

Charles Schuyler Schenck, who had also moved to Hollywood in the late 1920s to do some writing and lead an orchestra. Schenck was the grandson of a former bank president in Toledo. While he was not quite as rich as Jimmy Whiting, he was very handsome, and it was Schenck who eventually won over MacCloy's affections with his easygoing style and midwestern personality. He and MacCloy drove to Yuma, Arizona, where they eloped in November 1931. The *Toledo News Bee* headlined the story "June MacCloy Chooses Love Over Riches," framing it as a "cupid-wins-the-day" type story line, but this, too, proved to be just another Hollywood script headed for the scrapheap. Her marriage to Schenck lasted only a few years. By 1933, MacCloy was still a tender twenty-four years of age and had already been married and divorced three times.

It was the stuff of which gossip columns are made. The first of her unions was to an Atlantic City man by the name of Robert Forrester in 1928, which, according to the *Toledo News Bee*, had been annulled on application by MacCloy's mother within a year. Then the actress married a Cincinnati film salesman, Wilbur Guthlein, who divorced her in 1931, claiming she refused to give up her career and live with him. She told reporters that "yes, she did refuse to live with him because he was mentally cruel and he couldn't support her, so she had to make her own living." Within six months after their divorce, she would meet and marry bandleader Schenck of Toledo, only to get a Mexican divorce decree in 1933. She would marry once more in the 1930s to trumpeter Claude Harrison (Otts) Whiteman. The divorce was amicable and not her last attempt at matrimony. The man who did eventually win her heart for the long term was Neal Wendell Butler, a California architect who shared her love of jazz music and with whom she had two children. A statuette of Louis Armstrong was always prominently displayed in their living room. Shortly after her marriage in 1941, she retired from show business and made her home in Southern California. Peter Mintun, a jazz pianist who got to know June about ten years before she died said the once-famous actress would often fail to mention to others later in life that she ever had such a promising film career. Her reluctance to do so was probably rooted in an earlier belief that people of society looked down on those in the film industry.

Not much is known about June's later years, but it appears that she withdrew entirely from the whirlwind of celebrity and chose to live a quieter and more normal life as a mother and partner to her husband of the next forty-four years. Neal Butler passed away in 1985, and twenty years later, June Mary MacCloy Butler died of natural causes on May 5, 2005, in Sonoma, California, in a care facility at the age of ninety-five.

Following her death, in a special tribute to her, two of her films were showcased in 2005 at Film Forum in New York: *Reaching for the Moon* and the comedy *June Moon*—a final encore for a Toledo girl who made good.

Chapter 8

The "Luckey" Legend of Ben Stone

The black man's entry into the annals of American law enforcement really didn't begin to materialize until little over a century ago, in the late 1800s and early 1900s. Even then, the number of African American recruits was not great, occurring mostly in larger cities where black populations were also larger. In Toledo, Albert King was the first black citizen hired to wear a Toledo police badge, in 1900. In the smaller communities of the area, minority police officers were nowhere to be found, and in many communities, that is still the case.

So it was surprising to learn that the first black man in Ohio to become a small-town police chief was Ben Stone, in the tiny Wood County village of Luckey, Ohio, in the 1920s. He was born Benjamin Franklin Stone in 1874, of mixed Irish and African American parentage. While history doesn't record exactly where he was born, we do know that he and his brother, Tom Stone, eventually ended up in an orphanage on Lagrange Street in North Toledo. By the time he was ten years old, Ben and his brother had been taken from the orphanage by a farmer named Bill Dunipace, who needed help on his farm near Luckey. Dunipace was a bachelor and gave the brothers the promise of a better life in exchange for doing the various chores and jobs that needed to be tended to. Apparently, Tom Stone didn't take kindly to the idea of being part of the farm life. He fled back to Toledo, but Ben must have found something to his liking and stayed on to work with Dunipace. It was on that rural acreage that he lived out his childhood in the late 1800s. It is said that his relationship with Dunipace grew over the years, and they became more like father and son than farmer and farmhand. Two decades later, when Dunipace died, he left young Ben eighty acres of land and a house on Sugar Ridge Road. For a number of years, Ben tried his own hand at farming and living the rural lifestyle, but as a young man of about thirty years old, he wasn't content with the notion of settling down and working the land. He had other interests, and one of them was guns. Throughout his boyhood, he enjoyed shooting guns and spent much of his time while growing up honing his skills as a marksman. Locals say he became so good with a revolver that he could shoot the eye out of a crow perched in the highest branch of a tree. One neighbor says he actually saw Ben shoot at and hit the same nail head on a wooden door four times in a row. He also enjoyed other thrills like speed and motorcycles. He had a motorcycle and kept it parked at night inside his modest house on the farm property where he lived. Stories are still told of how Ben would blaze at high speeds down the backcountry roads of Webster Township on his motorcycle, "plinking" at prearranged roadside targets with great accuracy.

Eventually, in 1916, Ben furloughed himself from the farming life and sold off forty acres of his land to a neighbor but kept the old cabin and the other forty acres where he lived. He also took a few odd jobs working for other farmers in the area. His solid reputation for hard work and honesty paid other dividends when he took a full-time job as the night watchman for the Schwan furniture store and funeral home in Luckey, guarding the business from the growing number of Depression-era criminals who roamed the area looking for things to steal. A few other merchants also paid Ben to watch their stores at night, and soon he was officially appointed the town marshal. With that designation, he was allowed to carry a gun, and he patrolled Luckey's streets at night with a flashlight in one hand and a shotgun in the other. He also tucked a .45-caliber handgun into the side of his well-worn shaggy coveralls that made up his familiar uniform. It can be stated without argument that Ben was hardly a student of fashion. His unshaven and grizzly face and his disheveled appearance were not helped by his refusal to wear a glass eye after he had lost one in an accident many years before. His reason for not wearing the glass eye, he said, was that "it doesn't make me see any better." Ben was clearly a man of modest needs and means. After selling his cabin and the remaining forty acres in the country, he eventually made his home in the back storeroom of the old Schwan furniture store, where his bed was fashioned from empty wooden boxes used for burial vaults.

Locals say Ben would have made a good character in a movie. If ever there was a great opening scene, it might have been written about the quiet autumn day in 1933 when this mild-mannered and friendly marshal became a real-life action hero. As the tale is told from the 1981 Luckey centennial history book, the story unfolded on Thursday afternoon, September 28, 1933. John Landwehr, who worked at the Schwan furniture store, was washing the front windows when he noticed a man walk toward the Luckey Exchange Bank wearing a hunting coat. Another man was sitting in a parked car, acting nervous, on the street nearby. Sensing that something wasn't right, Landwehr and his sister ran to the back room of the furniture store to awaken Marshal Stone, who had been up all night patrolling the streets. When informed of what might be happening at the bank, Ben promptly rolled out of bed, put a six shooter in each pocket and picked up a double-barreled shotgun loaded with buckshot.

The historical narrative states, "He went out the back door of Schwans down the alley and through The Williamson's Garage and went down the sidewalk past the bank and waited in the stairway beside the barber shop." Meanwhile, the bandit had entered the bank and pointed a pistol at Harvey Helm, the cashier, and two others in the bank and demanded the money in the drawer. As Helm passed $344.98 to the bandit, he touched an alarm button that sounded in the telephone office and several other downtown stores. Then he and others were herded into a back room of the bank by the bandit, who fled out the front door. As he exited, he was greeted by the shotgun-wielding Marshal Ben Stone, who said, "Stop or I'll shoot!"

That's when Ben Stone says he heard "two cracks" from the robber's gun and then felt something "nip" his legs, and "that's when I let him have the right barrel and he went down in a heap." Someone shouted that the robber was going to fire again, at which point Ben not only fired the other barrel at the robber but also pumped three more bullets into him from his pistol. As soon as the gunfire erupted, the other man in the getaway car took off. Ben would recall later, "I'm pretty sorry I didn't get him too." He was later caught and sent to prison.

By this time, the normally quiet downtown main street in Luckey was flooding with people who came to view the aftermath of this violent bank robbery that ended badly for the suspect, as he lay mortally wounded and bleeding profusely from his wounds, while Marshal Stone dealt with the pain and bleeding from two bullet holes in his legs. One of the people who came to town that day to witness the scene was LaVeda Graening, who was a teenager at the time. In her nineties and living in Perrysburg, she remembered that day clearly as the crowd gathered around the dead bank robber sprawled out on the bloody street.

"My cousin called me and told me what was happening and I ran as fast as I could to get there. The streets were filled with people and people gathered around to see someone shot in the street. It was so public, seeing a body there. Just out in front of everybody. I don't want to be too descriptive, but when they took his shirt off, you know, you could see the wound in his chest. It was awful."

By this time, Ben Stone, who had suffered two gunshot wounds to the legs, was being transported by a local resident to Mercy Hospital in Toledo. Graening remembers that townspeople were concerned for Ben and sent get-well cards to the wounded marshal in hopes for his quick recovery: "Everybody liked Ben. He was a friendly man. I can still remember seeing that little smile of his. He used to have little sayings and called some of the girls and women in town his little 'Ain-gies,' or Angels. He loved children, he was like a Granpa to me."

LaVeda Graening's remembrances of Luckey's most famous lawman are shared by many. The legacy of this man remains indelibly etched into the historical accounts of the Wood County community as a local hero. This is an unlikely and unusual embrace of a black man in the lily-white farm country of Wood County made up predominantly of German and Swiss ancestry at a time when racial prejudice was still practiced openly in many communities. The open warmth that was shown to Ben during this era says a lot about the people of Luckey and says a lot about the character of Ben Stone and the effect he had on the people of the community.

"He was my dad's best friend," LaVeda Graening recalls, and she tells of how Ben's "bunkhouse" or quarters, where he used to sleep at night in the back of the mortuary, often became a social gathering place for the men of the town, who would get together on Saturday mornings to tell stories over a potbellied stove. Ben, who was regarded as the "town character," often took his share of good-natured ribbing from some of the men in town about his dress, his bib overalls and his happy-go-lucky lifestyle, but Ben, it is written, always took it in good stride and laughed with those who made the jokes. After the bank robbery and shooting in 1933, the townspeople of Luckey took Ben a little more seriously. Appreciative of the fact that he had put himself in harm's way to protect the town and residents, the citizens found a new sense of respect for Marshal Stone. In November 1933, a few months after the shooting, Ben Stone was the guest of honor at a testimonial dinner at the Grace Lutheran Church in Luckey, where 160 of his fellow townspeople thanked him for his courage and service to the town and presented him with a new gold deputy sheriff's badge with his name engraved on the back. They also presented him with a check for $150.

Another gift Ben received was surprising and offered a strange twist to the bank robbery saga. It was a letter of thanks from the mother of Glenn Saunders, the bank robber whom he had shot dead. Mrs. Saunders, of Columbus Grove, thanked Ben for killing her son, saying he had always been trouble and she and her husband were relieved that he wouldn't be causing any more trouble. She continued her communication with Ben over the years, and they often exchanged Christmas gifts.

Ben continued his duties for the next decade in his adopted home of Luckey, patrolling the streets with his guns tucked into the bib overalls and greeting his friends and residents every day with a familiar smile. After the shooting, however, he had to give up riding his bicycle because of the wounds he sustained in the shoot-out. He sold it to a young girl in town, Betty Landwehr, who had become one of his "Ain-gies," or Angels. Her mother paid for the bike with ten dozen cookies, delivered over a period of time. Betty rode the bike for many years before heading off to Bowling Green to college. Betty now lives in Florida and has very fond memories of Ben Stone, as do most of those fortunate enough to have known him.

When Ben died on August 27, 1943, of heart disease at the age of sixty-nine. Staying true to his simple desires of life, his remains were cremated and his ashes spread over the Webster Township Cemetery at Scotch Ridge. Today, one can find a grave marker among those of the other families and settlers of the area. And while the old dirty boots of Ben Stone no longer walk the streets of Luckey protecting its citizens at night, the footsteps of this young orphaned boy still echo on the streets of time.

Chapter 9
Tales of Toledo's Tenderloin

Once upon a time in Toledo, there was a place called the Tenderloin, a segregated area of businesses and homes near downtown where life was lived on the wild side. It was a place where one could buy most anything to satisfy the cravings of the flesh. If you wanted it, it was probably for sale. It was its own city, which operated independently of the laws that governed morals and vice in the city, and it was a seductive magnet for those who sought to live their lives on the tattered hems of society, if only for a few hours a week. This was the Toledo Tenderloin. It is gone now. The only remaining evidence of it are a few buildings and the stories committed to print. History researcher Doug Tracy has spent a considerable amount of time tracking those old stories of the "district" and what took place there. Part of his interest was personal, in that his great-grandfather, Toledo police detective Lewis B. Tracy, was the police officer in charge of keeping peace in the Tenderloin, maintaining the fragile balance of what was "allowed" and where to draw the lines of propriety in a neighborhood where little was considered "improper."

Toledo's Tenderloin was located in the general area of where the Mudhens play baseball these days, in the section of town called Hensville, roughly between Monroe and Lafayette and between St. Clair and Erie Streets. There are still bars and saloons there to this day, but to be sure, no longer will Hens fans be likely to find the small clusters of "immoral houses" nearby, or the gambling houses, or the poolrooms, or the cheap rooming houses where who-knows-what took place. Newspapers from that

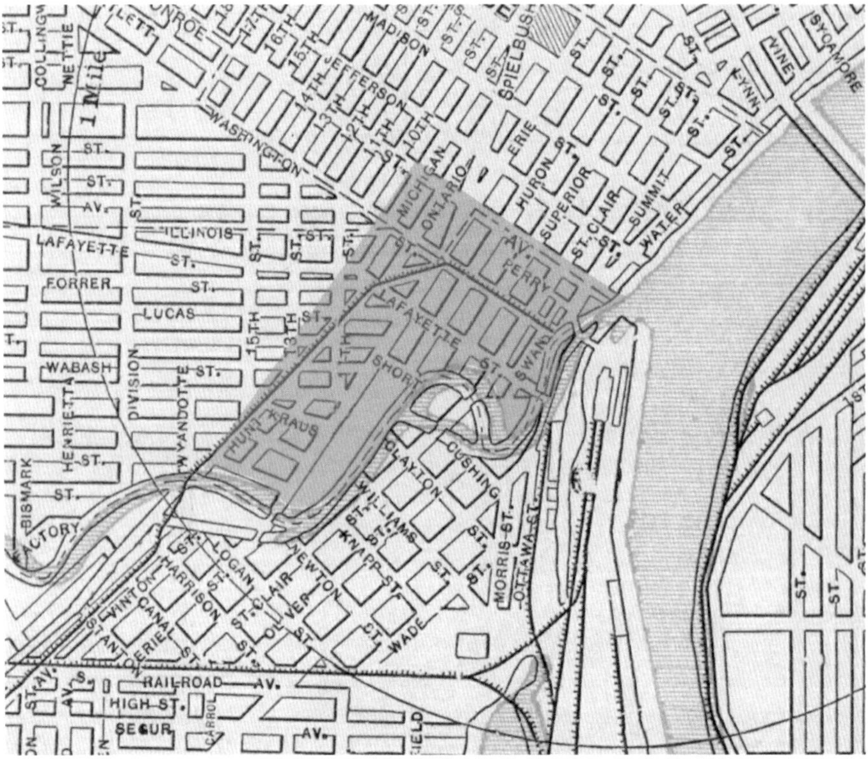

Map of the red-light/Tenderloin district in Toledo in 1902. *Doug Tracy Collection.*

era depict the Tenderloin as a derelict badlands where thieves, gamblers, grifters, ruffians, easy women and degenerates populated the streets. It is likely an accurate portrait.

Newspaper accounts of violence in the "district" were not uncommon, like this one from May 1904: "Toledo, O. May 2nd, Martin Duck, a Tenderloin bartender was shot through the heart by a Frank Williams. The latter arrested on a charge of murder. Williams claims he shot in self-defense."

Or this one from August 1911: "A Detroit man by the name of John Butler was shot at Lillian Rogers Saloon at 516 Lafayette Street in the heart of Toledo's tenderloin. He died an hour later at St. Vincent Hospital." Who killed Butler, or why, is still unknown.

The heyday of the notorious Tenderloin was sometime between the late 1800s and early 1900s, and during that period, the street might have been crowded with as many as thirty-five houses of ill repute in operation at any one time, with hundreds of so-called soiled doves waiting to sell their

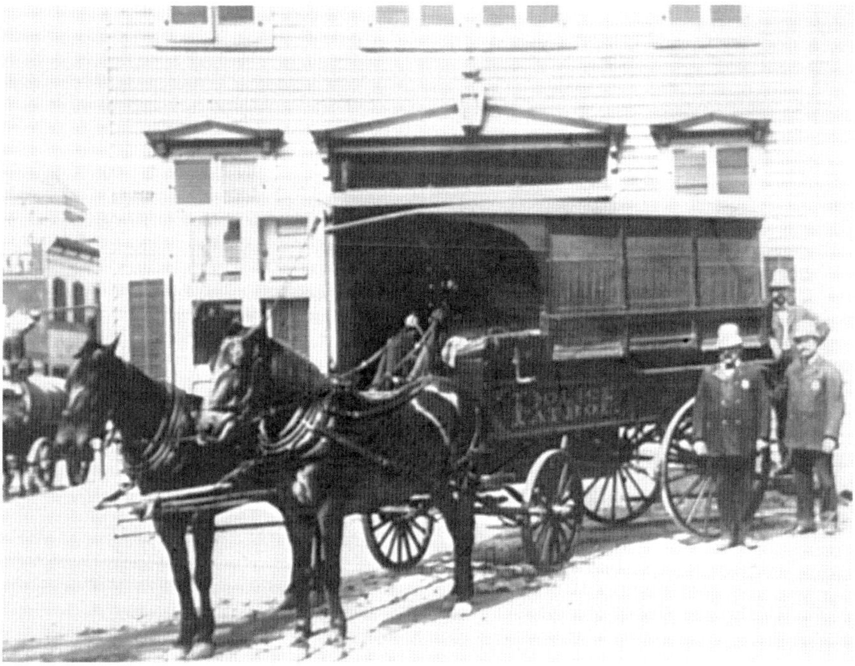

Police patrol wagons used by police in the Tenderloin. *Courtesy Toledo Police Museum.*

bodies. While most of the respectable citizens of the town knew this "Satan's den" was there, the efforts to clean it up had never been seriously employed and were never successful if they were undertaken. It might have just been considered an acceptable nuisance, as undoubtedly many of the respectable male citizens would find their way into that section to partake of activities to meet their needs, whatever they might be.

One of the well-known brothel keepers was Madam Nellie Schwinn. She was conducting business at her "resort" at 610 Lafayette Street toward the latter part of the district's era and was as colorful a character as any. Having been run out of Sandusky, Ohio, for running a "disorderly house" with her husband, Louis, she ended up in Toledo by about 1914. Nellie was not one to keep a low profile in the Tenderloin and gained some notoriety, as she became a regular name on the Toledo legal docket. She first accused a customer of stealing jewels and money from her and was later sued over a deal to buy a partnership in a movie house, and then in 1915, she and an accomplice, Harry Plummer, were charged with possession of 250 yards of silk taken from the Lakeshore Railroad in Toledo.

The trial became front-page news in many newspapers, as it was fodder for the tabloids that loved the seedy and sordid details of love gone wrong and lover-blaming-lover. The *Fort Wayne News* in Indiana reported on December 17, 1915:

> *To listen to the testimony in the government's case against Plummer is like hearing a recital from an old fashioned melodrama. The "wronged" woman, the "villain," the stolen "papers," and the love turned to hate are all there.*
>
> *Sordid, sickening, the details of her life of shame are poured without restraint by Nellie Schwinn into the ears of the court and the jury of twelve staid, elderly men, the majority of them farmers.*
>
> *Shrinking from the ordeal, yet feeling that only in this way can her score be righted, she tells her story without hesitancy, yet blushing over each shameful confession.*

During the one-week trial, Harry blamed Nellie and Nellie blamed Harry. Eventually, a deal was struck, with Nellie offering a full confession and testimony against Harry Plummer in return for a lesser sentence or, as it turned out, no sentence at all. Harry said Nellie gave him the silk as a birthday present. Nellie said Harry beat her, deceived her and threatened her if she didn't go along with his silk caper. The December 10, 1915 *Toledo Times* quoted Nellie: "I don't want him to die, but to live and repent his wrongs to so many. I have 50 pairs of shoes for myself, but never tried to sell any. He wore my robes about the house and I called him Nellie."

Harry ended up getting six years in Leavenworth Prison. Harry Plummer, it should be noted, had been running a saloon on Broadway Street in Toledo and was no stranger to the underworld. He had what were considered mob connections from his earlier days in Louisville, Kentucky, and he had made his share of enemies. Only one year before the silk caper, Harry and his wife, Kate (also the operator of a brothel in the Tenderloin), became front-page news when someone tried to kill him at his home. Four gunmen knocked on the door of his home on Oakwood, announced they had a "message from Louisville" and then shot him, once in the head and once in the leg. Harry's wife saw what was happening from the top of the stairs, grabbed a gun and started shooting. She killed one of the intruders. Harry Plummer would serve out almost all of his term of six years. During his time in prison, which he felt was unfair, his wife, Kate, died at the Toledo Hospital for the Insane. After his release from prison in 1920, he moved to Swanton, a small town west of Toledo, where he became a model citizen. He was head of the Republican Party in Fulton County and started Plummer Motors, which stayed in business there for many years.

Harry had obviously been the victim of Madam Nellie Schwinn's wicked ways, which was almost her signature as she grifted from town to town, making trouble and accusations while trying to extort money from anyone she could. One of her last victims in Toledo was a Toledo policeman. Lewis Tracy was the police guardian and guard over the district. In 1915, he was assigned to be in charge of the Tenderloin. It was a big job and a fragile one to keep the peace and maintain a balance of what was acceptable in an outlaw district, where many human indiscretions were tolerated in hopes that this "sin zone" would not spill over into the rest of the city. Tracy, who had an exemplary career as a detective and street officer, was a cop's cop. He was tough. Over his career, he was beaten up, robbed, shot, threatened and had bones broken, yet he remained dedicated to his work. Perhaps best of all, he was considered tough yet compassionate and fair.

Apparently, Nellie Schwinn saw another prey in the good-natured Tracy. In late 1915, the proud Detective Tracy and other officers were accused by Schwinn of taking bribes from the brothel keepers. Apparently in retaliation for raiding a brothel, she accused him of taking protection money from the owners of the "resorts" in exchange for tips about raids or other police activity in the area. The resultant grand jury hearings landed the front-page newspaper stories, which were filled with more seamy stories about life in the Tenderloin. Tracy was eventually exonerated of the charges that had been lodged against him by Schwinn, but the stress of the hearings almost killed him, and during work one day at the police station, he collapsed from exhaustion. It was the start of a health decline that never improved. Tracy tried to institute new policies and rules in the district and proposed to the city some ways to improve conditions for "dance hall proprietors and persons engaged in immoral business." The new rules included prohibition of dance music from Saturday midnight until Monday morning, outlawing outsiders from bringing liquor for "inmates" into resorts and a three-times-per-year limitation on changes of residency of "immoral women."

Historian Doug Tracy has done considerable research on his great-grandfather Lewis Tracy, from which much of this story has been derived. He also writes about the high regard that many in the Tenderloin had for Officer Lewis Tracy. "Tracy's job was to register, photograph and arrange regular health check-ups for all of the street-walkers, sporting ladies and brothel inmates in the Tenderloin. All were required to carry up-to-date

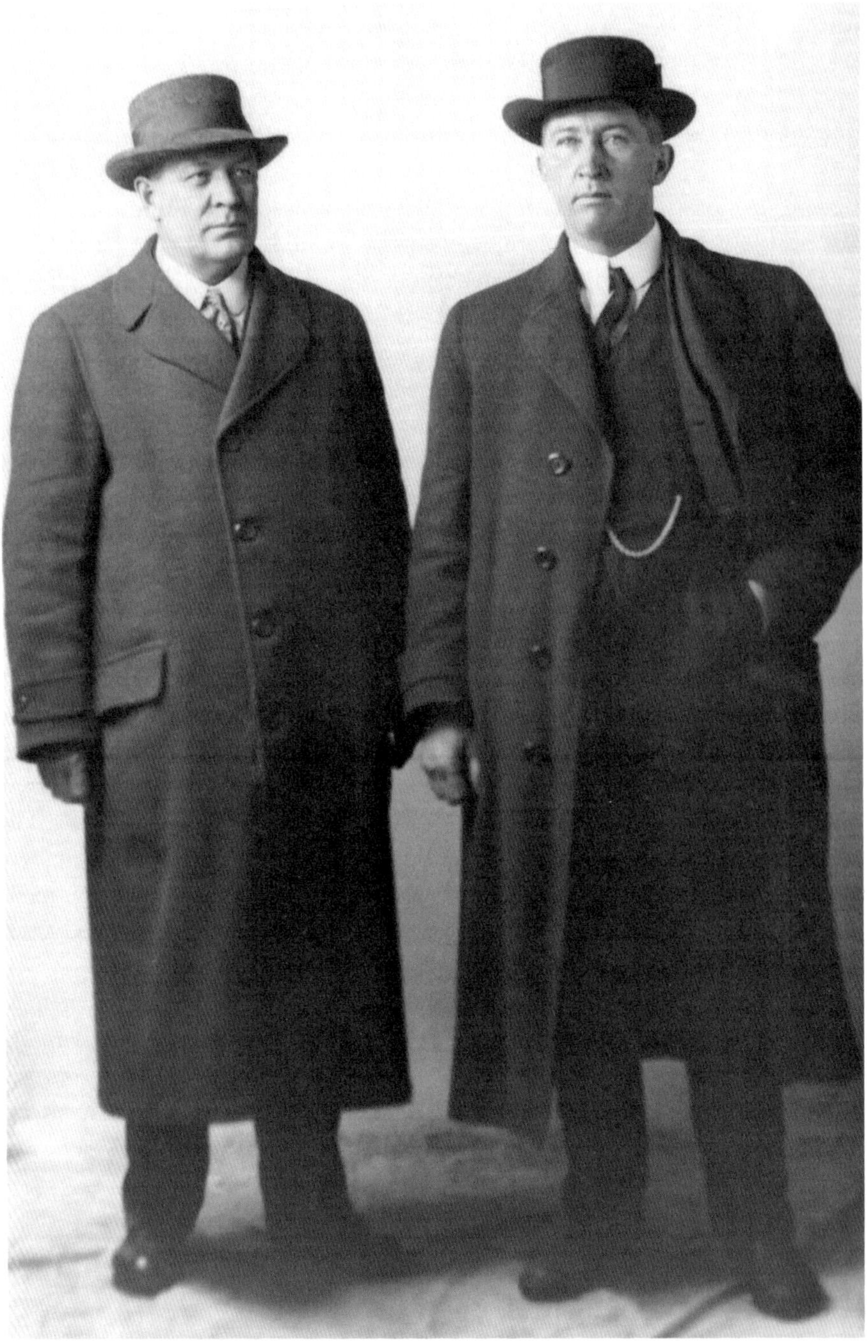

Detective Lewis Tracy (*left*). *Doug Tracy Collection.*

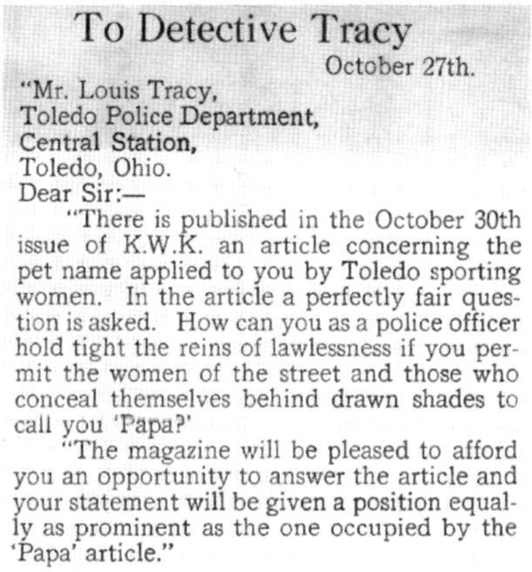

To Detective Tracy

October 27th.

"Mr. Louis Tracy,
Toledo Police Department,
Central Station,
Toledo, Ohio.
Dear Sir:—

"There is published in the October 30th issue of K.W.K. an article concerning the pet name applied to you by Toledo sporting women. In the article a perfectly fair question is asked. How can you as a police officer hold tight the reins of lawlessness if you permit the women of the street and those who conceal themselves behind drawn shades to call you 'Papa?'

"The magazine will be pleased to afford you an opportunity to answer the article and your statement will be given a position equally as prominent as the one occupied by the 'Papa' article."

The *Toledo News Bee* took issue with Detective Tracy being referred to as "Papa" by the brothel workers. *Toledo Public Library*.

health certificates. Tracy knew them all, and they all knew him. In time, the denizens of the Tenderloin developed a deep respect for the compassionate officer they came to know as 'Papa.'"

There were some voices of influence who did not take well to the "ladies" of the Tenderloin referring to the detective as "Papa." Editorials appeared that questioned this special relationship and certainly left a stain on Tracy's reputation. By 1918, a movement was afoot nationwide to begin a concerted campaign to shut down these "badlands" that were common in many American cities. One of the reasons stated were the effects of vice on the draft-age young men and factory workers supporting the war effort. As a result, there was external pressure from the federal government to protect potential soldiers from the ravages of vice, venereal disease and crime that might keep them out of the army. The urgent need to close the houses of ill repute had nothing to do with the social health and well-being of the women and girls who were sexually exploited there but more to do with patriotism.

And so, after decades of running twenty-four hours a day, catering to the wanton demands of humanity, the end of April 1918 was chosen as the deadline to bring down the curtain on Toledo's Tenderloin. On Tuesday, May 1, thirty-five resorts were closed up. As the *Toledo Blade* reported:

> *For the first night in years, excepting Sunday restrictions, the tinkle of the mechanical pianos and the skulking of women of the underworld, clandestine lovers, parasites, criminals, the occasional street fight or the back room brawl which brought policemen scampering, the coming and going of taxicabs with mysterious "fares," the savory odor of the sandwich man's wares—for the first night in years all of these were gone.*

It was estimated that approximately 1,365 ladies faced expulsion from the area, and there was great concern about what would become of them and their scandalous lifestyles. Community and religious groups, including the Florence Crittenton Home for Girls, offered to help them change their evil ways by finding legitimate jobs for those who wished to make an honest living. Many in the city were afraid of these "soiled" women mixing with the general society.

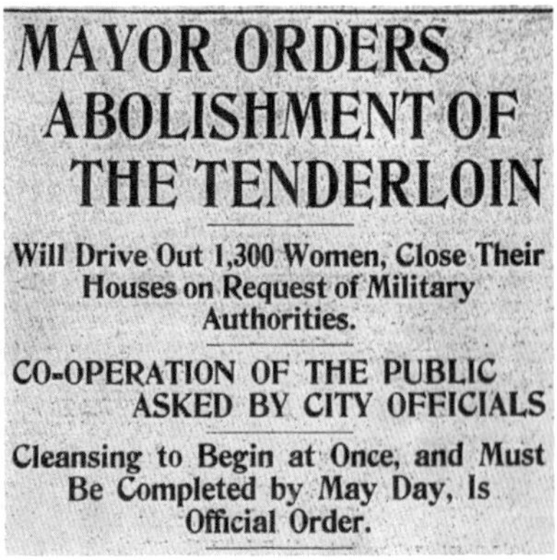

MAYOR ORDERS ABOLISHMENT OF THE TENDERLOIN

Will Drive Out 1,300 Women, Close Their Houses on Request of Military Authorities.

CO-OPERATION OF THE PUBLIC ASKED BY CITY OFFICIALS

Cleansing to Begin at Once, and Must Be Completed by May Day, Is Official Order.

The long-awaited closure of the Tenderloin couldn't come soon enough for many Toledoans. *Doug Tracy Collection.*

Health professionals were concerned that venereal disease might become epidemic, and they set up special clinics for check-ups and also monitored for scarlet fever, diphtheria and morphine addiction. In neighboring towns and villages, there was particular concern that eviction of Toledo's netherworld meant that the refugees would just migrate to other neighborhoods or surrounding towns.

The *Toledo Blade* reported that the proprietor of one resort at Superior and Lafayette Streets (now the location of the Spaghetti Warehouse) did not want to leave her house because it was filled with expensive furniture, carpets, draperies and masterpiece paintings. At St. Clair and Lafayette, the Fort Dixon Inn, which was reputed to also be a bordello, ceased those operations but continued business as a restaurant and museum of strange objects and curiosities. Some of the other sporting houses merely reopened as male-only saloons or boardinghouses.

As Doug Tracy notes from newspaper accounts, "As the May 1 deadline approached, activity in the vice zone increased dramatically, as much for the residents as for the curious citizenry." The Tenderloin became the center of attention and was visited by hundreds, if not thousands, of curious sightseers. Disturbances were numerous. The continuous clang of police automobile gongs could be heard from early Saturday night until Sunday morning. Long lines of automobiles filled the streets. Sidewalks were almost impassable, due to density of the curious. So heavy was travel, police were forced to station men on corners to act as traffic guides. The Tenderloin was busier than ever, and the *Toledo Times* headlined its story on the activity as "Slumming Open Doors of Sin":

> *In the last hours of their existence, the lights in Toledo's vice grottos shed a malevolent glow. The ghosts of myriad nights of ribaldry were abroad,*

> *patrolling for the last time the precincts where in times past they had appeared as living, flaunting things. Electric bulbs, once radiant, seemed to shimmer with a vixen-like glow, as the tapers of death, casting their last sad shadows over the figure of a corpse. They were the sepulchers of things which rest in the traditions of the underworld—fortunes won and lost, murders committed and forgotten, tragedies gossiped over and lost in the swirl of events "below the dead line."*

By midnight of Tuesday, May 1, a *Toledo News Bee* writer poignantly and poetically painted a picture of the final night of the Tenderloin:

> *Never before was the tenderloin utterly crushed out, although there had been minor restrictions imposed on it from time to time. The women of the underworld accepted the order as a matter of fact. Their exodus began several weeks ago, but not all of the resorts were abandoned before the ban became effective. Many sight-seers collected during the last hours on Tuesday night in such places as were still open. There was a little feverish revelry but the district in general was quiet. No better night could have been chosen for the passing of the tenderloin. Rain swept the streets where the refuse which had accompanied the moving-out of some of the places during the day, was still scattered. Thru the cold mist, the lights of passing autos made yellow halos and the electric globes above the doorways of the houses blinked in a sinister manner. A few men loitered along sheltering walls. Cats, abandoned in the Tuesday exodus of the women, slunk thru the rain. Houses, where a few nights before there had been music and laughter, were silent. By midnight the lights above the doors of the houses had all gone out. Behind drawn blinds even the lamps were darkened. Notorious resorts were deserted and lowered heavily over the dismal streets. The segregated district had passed.*

Chapter 10

The Clock that Never Stopped

The once scandalous Toledo Tenderloin was but a distant memory by the time Lillian Lewandowski bought the Farber Grille in Ottawa County in the early 1950s. But Lillian was a savvy businesswoman who understood the laws of supply and demand. She was fully cognizant that even though Toledo no longer offered an open marketplace of sex for sale, as there had been in the old days of the Tenderloin, there was still a demand for the services. She was quite right. The business she would operate on Woodville Road at the Ottawa and Wood County line was so popular, and so notorious, that it would became an enduring legend of mystery, sex, scandal and secrets—some that, no doubt, Lillian took to her grave.

Lillian Lewandowski was born in 1919 in Toledo's Polish neighborhood known as Kuschwantz (Koosh-vahntz). We don't know much about her early years, but we know that she was born to Joseph and Martha Lewandowski and was one of five sisters and a brother who, in the 1920s, were living in a modest home on Indiana Avenue. Their father was a World War I navy veteran. His parents had emigrated from Poland, and he was employed and worked as a truck driver. Lillian's mother was also Polish. One can only assume Lillian's life was typical of a girl growing up in the Prohibition era of the 1920s in a large Polish family existing under the roof of a small home. Probably a mix of Polish and English languages was spoken in the house, amid the pleasant aroma of traditional Polish food cooking on the stove. But perhaps not all was well in the home.

Lillian's son, adopted Michael Tailford, says something happened one day to turn Lillian's world upside down. When she was about eight years old, in 1927, coming home from school on a cold, rainy day in March, she found her father's body hanging in the garage, a victim of his own hand. She could still vividly recall much later in life that horrific moment and the scene of what she witnessed. This would have been a difficult and traumatic moment for anyone, especially an eight-year-old. How it affected her later sensibilities in life, no one can say.

The cruel reality did change for Lillian and her siblings, as two years later, their mother would marry Anthony Purol, who moved the family to his home on Humboldt Street. The 1930 census shows Lillian and her siblings living there with their mother and stepfather. They must have had some religious upbringing in the Catholic-centered Polish culture, as Lillian and some of her sisters were enrolled at Central Catholic High School, where her photo is found in a 1939 yearbook.

Michael Tailford, who lives in Arizona, is still attempting to put all the pieces together of his mother's life and how she came to become one of the area's most notorious madams. He says he knows in conversations with her that sometime in her teens, like many of that age, she left home and started living on her own. After she left school, she spent some time joining the war effort of World War II, painting nose art emblems on aircraft. She told Michael that she was good at it. Michael doesn't know for sure where she was living at that time, but records from city directories indicate she did live as a factory worker in Bay City, Michigan, in 1940–41. During that time, she was married to someone with the last name of Lane, and she traveled south to Jacksonville, Florida, under the name of Lillian Lane. It was there that she married a young naval aviator from the Jacksonville Air Station named Bud Davidson. Michael has a picture of him posing with a cigarette in his uniform that says, "To the prettiest girl this side of heaven. Bud." It's dated 1942. Marriage records show she married Bud on May 9, 1942.

The late 1940s brought Lillian back to Ohio, divorced from her Florida sweetheart, and by some twist of fate or fortune, she became engaged to Michael Pasco of Port Clinton. Pasco was the son of Rosie Schallo Pasco, perhaps the most well-known businesswoman in Port Clinton but one who was not invited to dine with the mayor or to afternoon business luncheons. Rose, an Italian American girl from New Jersey, was also known as "Dago Rosie," the operator of the largest and most openly run brothel from Cleveland to Chicago. It was known to the community and its customers as "Rosie's," offering services for men, young and old, that they couldn't get anywhere else in town. Rose and her gals were whispered about in this small Ottawa County town as they went about their lives, shopping, getting their hair done or eating at local restaurants. One man told this writer that his mother used to run one of the local hair salons and Rose was a regular customer, often bringing several of her charges with her for their regular beauty treatments and hair styling. If Rose Pasco was afraid of scandal, she didn't show it. And she was certainly not afraid to make sure that local police and politicians were "reimbursed" for their tolerance of her business, which operated from a large two-story frame house on Buckeye Boulevard on the east side of town. It became a regular and familiar haunt for the thousands of soldiers stationed at nearby Camp Perry during the war years. A retired local judge confided that "it was almost a necessity in a small town like Port Clinton, with so many single young soldiers around." The story of Rosie's spread far and wide in postwar years as the young soldiers took their memories of the place home with them, wherever that might be.

Lillian and Mike Pasco were married in 1947 while living in Bay City, Michigan, where Rose had returned following the end of the war in 1945. By then, Lillian was divorced and ready to start life anew. Two years after she and Mike Pasco married, they were living in Ottawa County and bought a home together just outside Elmore, in the western part of the county. The home was a low-slung type, made of concrete block and built in the modern style of a California Ranch. It was built near the Portage River on a large lot with a stone guest house and a small swimming quarry. It was a virtual compound made more mysterious and private by the tall wooden fence that surrounded it. Shortly after they purchased the home, they were forced to sell a large parcel of their land to accommodate the Ohio Turnpike, which ran adjacent to the property.

It was about this time that Lillian and Michael and Michael's mother, Rosie, decided to expand the family business. The war was over, and likely Rosie's was not hauling in the revenue it once was during the salad days of the '40s. The family story is that Rosie bought Farber's Grille and truck stop for Lillian and Michael, with intentions to offer more than bacon, eggs and coffee to weary truckers. Situated in Ottawa County, on County Line Road adjacent to Wood County, it was a mere ten miles from downtown Toledo, a straight twenty-minute drive out Woodville Road. This was an easy and quick route for a man who was hungry for love. And besides, Woodville Road already had a reputation as a mecca for gambling and juke joints. In the early 1950s, the eight-mile stretch of roadway from the town of Northwood to Genoa was home to at least ten roadhouses, a couple of illegal gambling spots, poker games, two or three truck stops with slot machines and a mostly shuttered and shabby amusement park (Forest Park) that was reputedly controlled by the Toledo mob. Vice did not take a holiday on Woodville Road. So why not add to the menu of options? That's exactly what Lillian Pasco did, as she and Michael transformed the grille they bought into the Round the Clock, or the Clock, as most locals began to call it. There was a two-story white frame building with a large gravel driveway and apron to accommodate the trucks and a large neon clock on the side of the second story. Its multicolored lights blinked round and round as a beacon to the weary and lonely.

It didn't take long before the gravel driveway was filled with cars and trucks on any given night of the week. Some of the customers walked through the front doors of the first floor to get a sandwich and a drink. Others moved furtively around the back side of the place to find the narrow and steep stairway that led to the more expensive menu on the second floor. The Clock would quickly rival Rosie's as the most popular brothel in northwest Ohio, or maybe the Midwest. For Lillian, though, tragedy struck her young life in 1955, when her husband, Michael Pasco, began having serious problems of heart failure. One night while he was lying in the hospital with a short time to live, Lillian was notified to come quickly, as Michael was fading. Her son, Mike, says his mom told him that she rushed to the hospital hoping she wouldn't be too late. As she got to the hospital and ran to his bedside, he was still alive. She grabbed his hand. He looked at her, closed his eyes and passed away. Mike, who was adopted later when she remarried, was named for her husband Michael.

The Clock would continue to operate twenty-four hours a day, raking in tidy sums of cash and allowing Lillian to live a very comfortable and sometimes lavish lifestyle. Mike says she enjoyed entertaining. "She was the life of the party" and loved to throw parties and dinners, giving her guests only the best. Talented in the kitchen, she would serve everything from escargot to the best steaks and wines. "She was a very loving and giving person, despite her reputation; that's what many people don't know about her," says Mike, who lived close to her in Arizona in her later years. He says she was very kind and loved to give gifts to people. That was the way she showed her love.

Because of the Clock's proximity to Genoa, this writer, who grew up there, became familiar with it as a boy, hearing the rumors and stories of what took place there. As a teenager, I would meet Lillian while I was working as a carryout and delivery boy at a popular Genoa grocery store. It was the place where Lillian and her two young children, a boy (Mike) and a girl, often shopped for food and wines, either for her large ranch home near Elmore or for the women who worked and stayed at the Clock. It was my job, at times, to deliver groceries to both locations, as I was instructed to follow her in her flashy new Cadillac convertible so she could unlock the security gates to their sleek California-style home. Sometimes, I would be instructed to carry the sacks of groceries up the long narrow staircase to the second floor to the waiting ladies at the Clock. As a result of this appointed duty, my education in the ways of the world began early in life. It was always difficult for me to believe that the local law enforcement agencies didn't know what was going on there, when as a sixteen-year-old, I knew, as did everybody else.

So many people knew about the Clock that few were surprised when, in 1970, federal agents raided the "truck stop" along the highway and brought down the curtains on Lillian's notorious Clock. After almost twenty years in operation, Lillian's troubles would multiply quickly. She and a small army of accomplices were facing major federal indictments of numerous charges, including tax evasion, gambling, white slavery and bribery. It was a case that captured the public's attention, offering a trial filled with steamy testimony and revealing the sordid underbelly of the prostitution trade and how the Round the Clock Grille, the front for a popular bordello, was able to evade criminal prosecution for so many years. The stunning revelations opened the floodgates of a criminal enterprise that had many connections. The testimony and evidence would eventually bring down the sitting Ottawa County sheriff, James Ellenberger, for accepting thousands of dollars in bribes. It would send former Ottawa County sheriff Myron Hetrick to prison for perjury when he lied about helping to distribute the bribe money. Others were involved in other aspects, like transporting women across state lines.

At the center of the stormy scandal, of course, was Lillian, the striking strawberry blonde known by many simply as "Ginger." Also in the center of the storm was Lillian's former mother-in-law, "Dago" Rose Pasco, as she was also indicted, along with her daughter Janet Terry, who helped run the Clock; a woman by the name of Nancy Maxwell Scott, the owner of the building; and her partner, "Holy Joe" D'Angelo. It was an ensemble of characters straight from "Central Casting." It was the stuff of movies and tabloids.

The federal agencies that developed the case against the Clock had done their homework and had been investigating the activities there for many years as part of an ongoing probe into organized crime in the Toledo area. While there were certainly other larger targets in the investigation, it was

Lillian who took the major heat and the eventual fall, pleading guilty to tax evasion and a charge of white slavery (transporting women across state lines for immoral purposes). Her convictions netted her a four-year term at a women's federal prison facility in West Virginia, plus a fine of hundreds of thousands of dollars. Whatever she had accumulated in wealth over the years was gone—wiped out in the blink of an eye and a federal tax lien. Not only had she lost the house in Elmore, but she had also lost a small mansion that she and her then husband, businessman Lew Tailford, had purchased in Paradise Valley, Arizona. It was a beautiful luxury home where Lillian would escape to in the cold winter months and a place where her attorney had advised her to live a few years before the raid. Her son, Mike, says they lived there as her official residence for a long time and would visit Ohio on occasion. She was residing in Arizona when federal agents stormed the Clock in the infamous raid. The federal prosecutor in the case, John Connely, says the investigation they were conducting at the time in Toledo gained greater priority and a new impetus after Lillian did an interview with a Phoenix newspaper for a feature on her new house in Paradise Valley. The article set off alarm bells with IRS agents in Phoenix because Lillian told the reporter that her lavish lifestyle was made possible because she ran a "truck stop" in Ohio.

The highly publicized trial in Toledo resulted in plenty of headlines and many convictions. Lillian tried for a while to get an early release from the West Virginia lock-up so she could take care of her "adopted" children, but the courts didn't buy it. So she served out her term, crocheting and reading and helping other women learn to read. Her adopted children stayed with Lew Tailford. After her release, Lillian returned to freedom but was left with little in the way of any material wealth. The homes were gone, including the Arizona house, which had featured a two-thousand-square-foot master bedroom, a circular bed, exquisite furnishings, paintings and sculptures. "She loved money," says Mike. It was hard for her to accept that she had nothing anymore, and she was "bitter about it" in her later years. But the Polish girl from Toledo persevered. She needed a new life and a new income, so Mike says she studied to become a respiratory therapist and then worked well into her late seventies before officially retiring. She still owed the IRS a small fortune and would laugh when her small tax refunds would be confiscated every year to pay off her IRS debt, which was estimated to be about $1 million by the time she died. In the final years of her life, the once vibrant woman with a lust for life began to falter. The light of her being began to dim, and like the neon clock on her famous house of ill repute, it finally blinked out. In a nursing home facility and in failing health, in 2009, she passed away peacefully at the age of eighty-nine. She took her secrets with her.

Mike says he has learned a lot about his adoptive mother in recent years but knows there are things he may never know. He has a box of old photos and some dusty films that his mother left him. He even has the full transcript of the famous Toledo trial that packed the gallery of the federal courthouse for several months in 1972. There are few people he can ask who were around. His mother preferred not to talk about it and rarely, if ever, told her co-workers or friends in the Phoenix area. Mike says she told him, "After I die, you can tell the world." He is still trying to figure out what to tell.

When you drive by the corner of Woodville and County Line Road today, the old Round the Clock Grille is long gone. Erased from the landscape by a ball of flame shortly after its closing, the land was taken over and replaced with a bank. And yes, many do see some irony there. However, little or nothing lingers to remind us or future generations of what took place there. How, for so many nights and years, the parking lot at this rural outpost of sin would be filled with a fleet of yellow taxicabs from Toledo that brought out men by the thousands. The cabs would wait in the shadow of the glowing red hand on the big neon clock on the outside of the building as it blinked round and round in circles, almost daring the outside world to come in and indulge in a moment of worldly pleasure.

But now, decades later, the cabs are gone and the Clock has stopped, seen only in the minds of those who remember.

Chapter II

East Toledo's Man of Trees

You've probably never heard of Louis Hirschy. But if you live in East Toledo or spend any time there, just look up and you might behold the progeny of his passion. His works of art, if you will. For Louis Hirschy was a sculptor, an artist of landscape, and his medium was trees. Lots of them. This mostly forgotten Swiss immigrant who arrived in Toledo in the latter part of the nineteenth century is credited with planting a forest of trees in East Toledo. Thousands of trees helped to create an urban woodland on the east side of the river. These giants of maple, oak, elm and sycamore were planted one by one, year and after year, with Hirschy's hand guiding each root into the earth with a love of nature that was deep and reverent. More than a century later, many of those trees, or their offspring, still live and tower above the streets as a living legacy to this "Man of Trees."

So who was Louis Hirschy, and why did he do this? According to what few articles have been written about him, Hirschy came to the United States from Switzerland at an early age in about 1875 and lived initially in eastern Indiana, where he worked at various jobs and attended college at Valparaiso University. By 1900, he and his wife, Louise, had relocated to Toledo, settling into a wooden two-story home at 503 Fifth Street near Greenwood in East Toledo. Hirschy, despite his academic training and literary background, worked for a number of years at the *Toledo News Bee* selling subscriptions and later took a job at the Toledo Shipyards on Front Street as a laborer. That is where he earned a living for the rest of his life.

Working at manual labor in a shipyard may seem an odd career choice for a man like Louis Hirschy, who was as enamored with books and literature as he was with trees and nature. In his 1936 obituary in the *Toledo News Bee*, he was called a "student of world literature" who was surrounded by one thousand books in the study of his home. It was in that beloved library where he was found dead by his two sons at the age of seventy-eight.

One of those books in his library was a cherished and rare Zurich Bible, printed in 1531, which he obtained while selling Bibles in Indiana during his youth, gladly trading one of his new Bibles for the early German-language Zurich Bible. The farmer who traded it thought it old and useless, as it was written in German. Hirschy saw it as something rare and of great value. He was correct, of course, for the Zurich Bible was the first printed Bible in recorded history. It is a rare and precious example of early printing. Family members who inherited the book thankfully thought it should be shared with the rest of the world, so they gave it to the Toledo Public Library. It now resides in the Rare Books collection and can be viewed upon request. It is the oldest printed book in the library's collection and may well be one of the oldest Bibles in the United States. There are even some handwritten notes in it from Hirschy about the Bible's contents, and those who view the five-hundred-year old tome will find scores of stunning and rare block wood-cut illustrations from the famous German artist Hans Holbein, who was also the personal painter for King Henry VIII.

Hirschy also appeared to be a student of evolutionist Charles Darwin. In fact, he was such an ardent supporter of Darwin's theories of natural selection that this East Toledo shipyard worker published several scholarly articles in 1902 in defense of Darwin's controversial writings. So perhaps it is not surprising that Hirschy also embraced a love of trees and nature that went far beyond a casual hobby. An article published in the *News Bee* in 1923 called Hirschy East Toledo's "Man of Trees" and praised his passion for tree planting like this: "To Hirschy, trees are a religion. They are his friends and his companions. Almost it seems they talk to him of their troubles and they answer to his care by growing straight and tall."

If you walk the neighborhoods around Hirschy's old house on Greenwood Street, you can still see many of those old trees, now thick and tall and gnarled with age, planted as saplings by Hirschy himself. Also still standing is Hirschy's home, which is not much more than a remnant of a distant past. Gone are the flowers and shrubs and the small "Garden of Eden" that he nurtured on the property. It was in this verdant paradise he created where Hirschy was said to have frequently retreated with a good book to read.

Today, his sanctuary of nature is gone. But for a few ancient vines twisted around a fence, the only other vestige of his private bower of greenery is the stump of an old sycamore that he once planted and took great pride in. He was so proud of this towering tree that he made his complaint heard at Toledo City Hall after overhead linemen cut away large sections of its upper branches in 1923. To Hirschy, this was nothing less than an act of desecration and sacrilege. The axes of the workers had ruined the symmetry of the giant branches aloft, and the normally even-tempered tree man let the mayor know of his disgust for what the workers had done. That towering sycamore, by the way, survived its maiming and lived into the twenty-first century and didn't feel the blade of a chainsaw again until 2007, when it was reduced to a rotting old stump between sidewalk and street, shorn off by the teeth of a chainsaw. Many of those trees he planted along Walden and Greenwood Avenues have suffered the same fate of time.

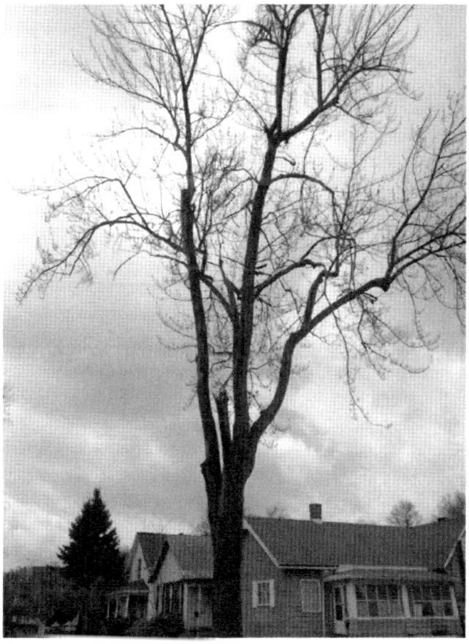

One of the many trees planted by Louis Hirschy still towers over the streets of East Toledo. *Author's collection.*

These were the last of the big giants of nature that formed a perennial summer canopy of shade for decades over this area of town. There is one thing, however, that Louis Hirschy did plant that will likely live longer than the trees. It is not a tree, not a shrub, not a flower but a "seed" harvested from the arbor of literature, that being the name of the street where he lived. When Hirschy moved to the neighborhood in 1894, it was still a rural crossroads, and Walden Street was called Fifth Street. But because of his appreciation for the writings of Henry David Thoreau about Walden Pond, Louis Hirschy, along with other neighbors, went to Toledo City Council in 1905 and requested the name of his street be changed from Fifth Street to Walden Street. Council approved the idea. From then on, 503 Walden Street is where Hirschy called home and lived out the balance of his abundant life—specifically, at the corner of Walden and Greenwood, a fitting name and place for Toledo's "Man of Trees."

Chapter 12

Major Charles Roth

The Badge and the Baton Story

The Toledo Symphony Orchestra holds a special place in the hearts of Toledo residents, as tens of thousands of Toledoans have been enjoying its masterful performances for almost eighty years. But what many symphony patrons may not know is the origins of the current symphony are rooted in the most unlikely of places: the Toledo Police Department. Namely, one officer: Major Charles Roth, a tough, no-nonsense, by-the-book old-style cop and undoubtedly one of the most colorful officers to ever wear a Toledo police badge.

The story began back in the early 1900s, when Roth was growing up in rural Defiance County. He was the son of a farmer who was killed while logging when the young Roth was just a boy. Roth worked the family farm as a lad and went to school but was not content with the notion of someday taking over the family farm. What Roth really wanted to cultivate was not crops but his love for music. It was the music in his heart that he heard, and by the time he was just eight years old, he had already taken up the piano, trumpet and numerous other instruments. He was gifted as a musician and loved playing music so much that his boyhood dream was to leave the farm behind and go to the big city of Toledo, where he might be able to play in the popular Toledo Police Band. In about 1915, with an eighth-grade education and some talent, Roth packed up his belongings and his instruments and followed his dream. He spent a couple of years as a barber in Toledo, but by 1917, he had joined the ranks of the police department as a rookie on street patrol, and when he wasn't walking the beat, young Roth was keeping the

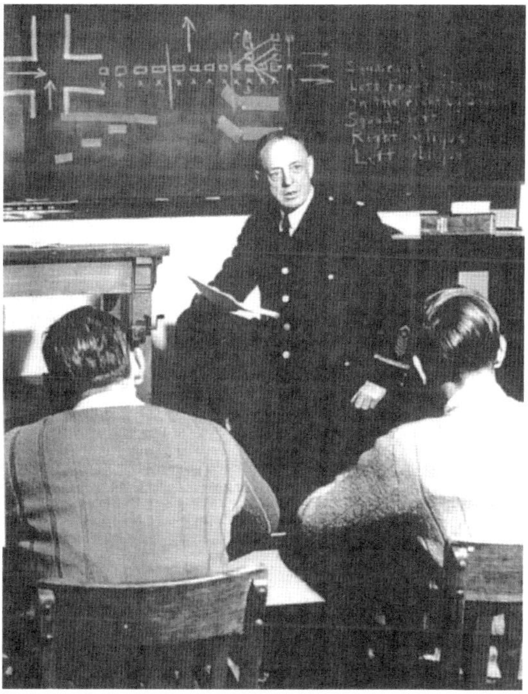

Right: Roth teaching classes at Toledo Police Academy. *Courtesy Toledo Police Museum.*

Below: Major Roth was considered a strict, by-the-book commander in the police department. *Courtesy Toledo Police Museum.*

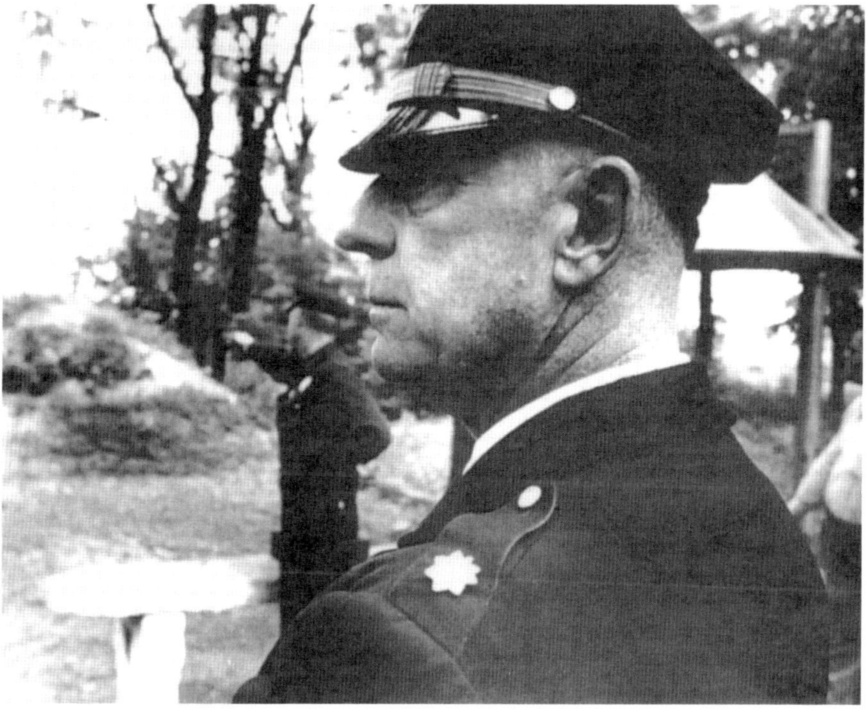

beat, practicing his music. True to his calling, the young man from Defiance County found his way into the Toledo Police Band, a popular music group of the era, always in demand at area events and parades. Roth had realized his boyhood dream.

Within a few years, though, Roth was not satisfied with the pedestrian repertoire of the police band. His ambitions to be a more serious musician were tugging at him. The popular songs and familiar marches of the era were too easy and predictable. The challenge of a symphonic orchestra is what he wanted to pursue, so in 1923, with no symphony in existence in the city, Roth saw an opportunity and organized the Toledo Police Civic Symphony. With a small group of eight police musicians, he widened the search for others and recruited musicians, amateurs and professionals from all walks of life. Wearing his blue uniform during the day and a black tuxedo at night, Roth would lead this new civic orchestra as its conductor and musical director for the next eighteen years.

The Toledo Civic Symphony scored high marks with many local citizens during the 1920s and '30s, appearing often in concert at numerous venues around the city. The former Devilbiss High School Auditorium was the group's "home" venue, although they performed at other locations and in other cities. Roth, as the conductor, reached for new horizons as a writer and composer. In fact, throughout his time with the symphony, he composed seventy-nine musical pieces, many of them scored for full orchestral treatment. In 1937, he wrote the official Centennial March for Toledo's 100th birthday that year. The orchestra debuted this original composition at the newly built Toledo Zoo Amphitheater. In an article from the *Toledo Blade* in 1992, Eric Liljequist, a former member of the Civic Symphony, remembers Roth as a good musician and a fine gentleman. He said Roth was not Arturo Toscanini, but "we were not the New York Philharmonic."

Roth's musical influences also were heard at home and in his private life. He was married to Blanche McKnight, a woman who was considered a serious concert pianist. She was so talented, according to a story told by her daughter, that when she was young, her mentors wanted her to tour Europe, but she opted to stay in Toledo.

By 1938, the leaders of the Toledo Civic Symphony decided to change its name and organizational structure. It was rechartered as the Toledo Symphony Orchestra. It continued to enjoy a positive reputation among many music lovers of the city and region. But as the city grew and began to climb out of the depths of the recession, some voices began to express the sentiment that Toledo needed a professional orchestra with a more

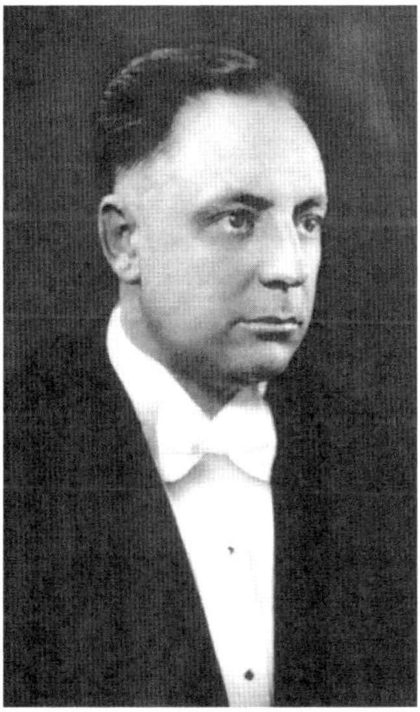

Major Roth as symphony conductor. *Courtesy Toledo Police Museum.*

accomplished musical director, not a part-time policeman leading an earnest group of amateurs. By 1940, another symphony was organized, and within a few years, the baton was passed, as maestro Charles Roth handed over his role and the name of the orchestra to the new conductor and the new symphony, which still continues the music tradition that was started by a Toledo policeman.

While music was the melody that played in Roth's life, it was always in harmony with other aspects of his life and career. Roth was not just a musician but had been building a formidable career on the streets as a Toledo police officer—a very good one. He made sergeant by 1928 and gained a reputation as being a very strict and precise taskmaster, often reprimanding patrolmen for the slightest infraction of rules. Stories are legend about Roth verbally chiding patrolmen for not buttoning up their coats while on duty or not filling out paperwork correctly. One longtime Toledo policeman said that when he was a young rookie, Roth told him one day that he would never be a good cop and that he should quit and find a different career. Roth's disparagement only galvanized the young man's determination to prove Roth wrong, and he stayed with the Toledo Police Department for the rest of his life.

Despite Roth's abrasive style and gruff demeanor, he is frequently remembered as the man who brought professionalism to the police department. One of his many legacies is the Toledo Police Academy. Up until the 1930s, police training in Toledo was minimal. It often consisted of walking a beat with a fellow officer for a few days and then getting turned loose as a rookie. The academy would change that, as Roth and his counterparts developed a program to pursue a more professional approach to training and standards. Roth personally authored several training manuals and codified the rules, procedures and ethics that policemen should follow. When he was not writing, he was teaching, working as an instructor in the new academy, where he was said to have trained 1,067 cadets over his career. He was the education director at the Toledo Police Academy, of which he was very proud. In a 1953 letter he wrote to a national syndicated

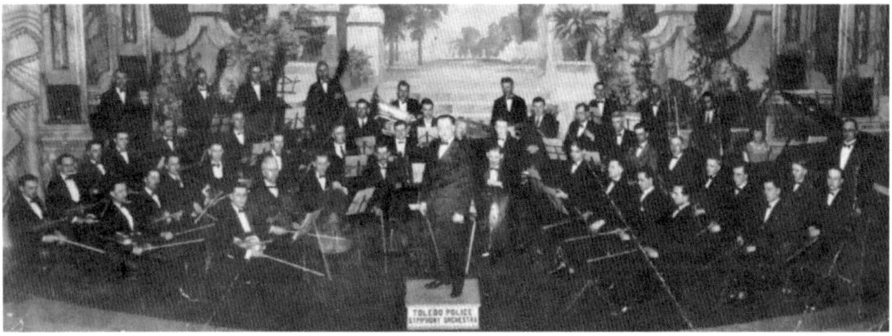

Charles Roth with Toledo Civic Symphony at Devilbiss High School. *Courtesy Toledo Police Museum.*

columnist, Roth detailed the extensive training that Toledo police cadets were offered in a variety of subjects, including criminal justice, history, English, psychology and forensics. He wrote, "The average college graduate will blush with shame at his own lack of practical knowledge when he realizes that policemen receive special instruction in criminal pathology including autopsies and special courses by the coroner." After his article appeared across the nation, Major Roth was invited to speak at numerous events about the special training that Toledo's police officers receive.

As the chief instructor and architect of the Toledo Police Academy, he rose to the rank of major, or "inspector." It was a top role in the department, and he might have become the chief, but it was said by his daughter that he never wanted to be chief of police because it was too political. Roth was not one to play politics, preferring instead to speak his mind on issues that he felt strongly about, no matter to whom he was speaking. He worked his influence in other ways. For example, this Renaissance man with a badge would literally redesign the badge of the police department. In 1938, he created the so-called Roth Metropolitan Shield that Toledo police officers wear today on their uniforms and hats. It featured the familiar three figures on Fallen Timbers statue image. At the time it was being considered, Roth pointed out to city council members in 1938 that Toledo was now a major city and should have a badge to reflect its prominence. He told the council, "We want to come to the metropolitan idea of design used by Milwaukee, New York and other large cities." It was given approval by council, but the city couldn't afford to replace the badge in 1938. Another twenty years would pass before the city found the funding, and in 1959, the badge became standard issue for the uniform and hat piece.

Another priority for Major Roth was to see that all officers had the training to excel at marksmanship. As Roth had been involved with his symphony, he was also working side by side with fellow officers in the 1920s and '30s to develop the Toledo Police Gun Range at the Detwiler marsh. The one-hundred-acre range near Bay View Park quickly became one of the largest and most effective firearms training courses in the United States. Roth played a key role in its development and conducted many of the marksmanship and gun-handling courses at the range, which held the envy of many police departments throughout the nation. It featured not just targets but also an officer-built range house, a concrete shooting backstop, a road course for teaching officers how to shoot from moving vehicles and moving mechanical targets on tracks. During its heyday, it was the go-to range for regular shooting matches, local, regional and national in scope. It even merited a write-up in *Look* magazine. Roth was a regular presence at the range, not only in the role of instructor but as a shooter, for he himself was an expert marksman. His renowned abilities as

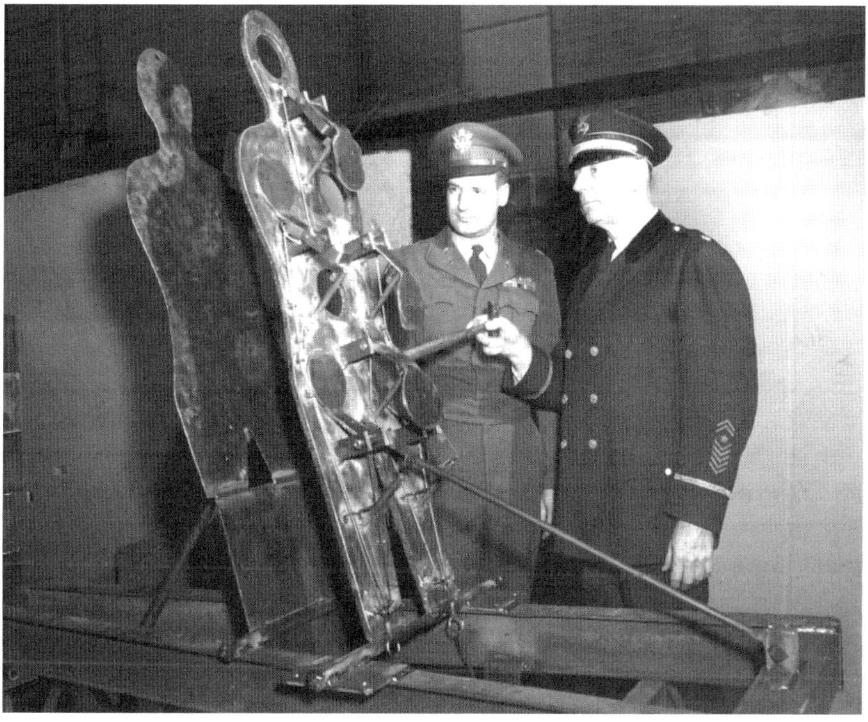

Inspector Roth examining a mechanical target with another officer. *Courtesy Toledo Police Museum.*

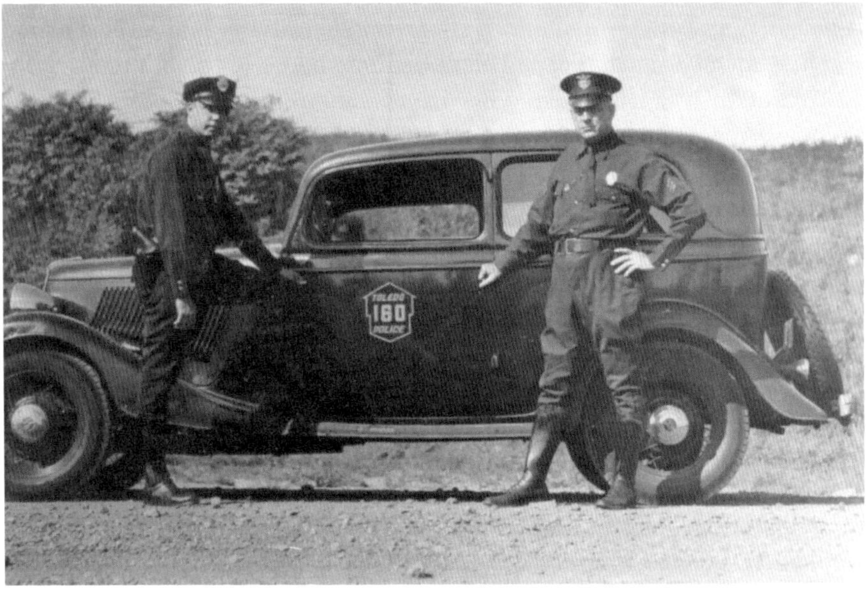

Roth and fellow officer Bosch standing in front of an early patrol car. *Courtesy Toledo Police Museum.*

a sharpshooter were unrivaled in Toledo and much of the nation. In 1927, he won the U.S. National Revolver Championship held annually at Camp Perry in Ottawa County. He shot a 272 out of a possible 300 points, just one point away from setting a world record.

And if Charles Roth did not have enough challenges and interests in life to keep himself busy, he also loved horses and developed an expertise in handling them. Having grown up on a farm in Defiance County around horses, he got to know, respect and ride them. He penned several books about horsemanship and was often invited to be the announcer for local rodeos. In his spare time, Roth taught Sunday school for a Methodist church. The résumé of Charles Roth was long and complex; he was a man of many talents. And while many knew and recall Roth as a strict disciplinarian, sharply candid and rarely shy to voice an opinion, those who knew him well say he could also be as compassionate as he was stern.

During the Depression years of the 1930s, Roth volunteered to become the music supervisor for the local WPA (Works Project Administration) music program, helping to find jobs for unemployed musicians. It was said that often he gave his musicians and fellow officers personal loans if they didn't have enough money to make it to payday. And while he might bring some officers up on charges for breaking the department rules, he would frequently plead for leniency in any punishment doled out to them.

By the end of his forty-five-year career with the Toledo police in 1962, Charles W. Roth had helped the Toledo Police Department grow as a professional law enforcement organization. He is credited not only with the founding of the Toledo Police Academy but also starting the crime prevention and missing persons bureau in the department. Five years after he retired, in 1967, Roth died at the age of seventy-six at St. Vincent Hospital after a long illness. But the music in his heart plays with every flourish of the conductor's baton at the Toledo Symphony Orchestra.

Chapter 13

The Remarkable Lost-and-Found Story of Lillie Bowers

Genoa, Ohio, in Ottawa County, is a quiet village. About ten miles south and east of Toledo, it's a well-known crossroads but is not witness to many big news happening within its limits, so rarely does it make the front page. It did so once for the deadly tornado in 1920 and another time for a sensational bank robbery a few years later when, during some sudden gun play on Main Street, the local druggist was shot to death. But day to day, Genoa is like many small dots on the Ohio map that never get much attention. Genoa did have one event that was the biggest local story that ever sent ripples beyond its village borders. It was a sensational story but one that few people today have ever heard of—a story so dramatic that if it were to occur today, Genoa would likely have to endure a crush of TV crews and cameras crowding one another to get the scoop. But there were no TV cameras back in the 1800s, just newspapers. And while the papers did report this story, for some reason, its notoriety faded with time like the ink on the old newsprint.

The roots of this curious tale began to unfold in 1867 in the Lake Erie port city of Sandusky, Ohio, with the kidnapping of a young three-year-old girl by the name of Marie Lillie Bowers. From family records, it is written that on October 26, 1867, a neighbor asked Martha Bowers if it would be okay if her three-year-old daughter, Marie Lillie, came to their house next door for a while to play. Her mother agreed, and so Lillie left with the neighbor woman. She heard her daughter say as she walked through the gate, "Lena, did you hear the 'histle blow?" Little did Mrs. Bowers know how much that utterance would mean to her.

About a half hour after Lillie left, her mother went to the neighbor's house to get Lillie, but the neighbor woman said Lillie had left on her own to head for home. They looked outside and up and down the street, but she was not to be seen. They called for her, and she didn't answer. An immediate and wider search was conducted by her frantic family members and neighbors, to no avail. By the next day, much of the city had become alerted and involved in the search. It was recounted in family records that every "vault and cistern" was searched, and even nearby "Sandusky Bay" was dragged for her body, but not a "single clue" turned up. Days went by, and there was still no sign of Marie Lillie Bowers. Everyone was sympathetic as townsfolk tried to locate the missing girl. Railroads even offered free passes to the distraught Bowers parents to help them in their search. Most of the major newspapers of the time carried the story of the missing child and the desperate search by her parents, James and Martha Bowers, to find their "Lillie." Many of the stories speculated that she had perhaps been abducted by a group of "gypsies" who were camped nearby, but nothing of substance ever turned up in support of that theory. The Bowers family suffered an agonizing wait. The long days passed into weeks and then months. Lillie was gone. The house was quiet. Mr. Bowers, a ship builder, for years later would buy advertisements in papers around the country in a vain attempt to find his daughter. One read:

> *Child Lost. The father of the little girl who was disappeared from Sandusky a short time since, has offered a one-thousand dollar reward for her recovery. The advertisement is as follows: One thousand dollars will be paid who can deliver to me my child alive, Marie Lillie, who was stolen from its home 52 Camp St., Sandusky on the 26th of October last. Is three years old of full flesh, light hair and blue eyes and when lost wore dark calico dress and check apron; is left handed, has a scar on the bottom of one of her feet, a nail on her left big toe was bruised. The money will be paid and no questions will be asked.*
>
> *James I. Bowers*

The Bowers family ran the ads for years in numerous papers across the country, but to no success. Some leads were reported and followed, but in the end, all proved to be false.

The only clues came in rumors and theories. The Bowers family even contacted Levi Stanley, the "King of the Gypsies," living in Dayton, and asked that he become involved, thinking he might be able to find out if any of "his people" had the child. Stanley reportedly became angry with the suggestion, although a child was brought forward as a possible candidate for the missing Lillie, but after Mrs. Bowers saw the girl, she knew it wasn't her daughter.

The Bowers family, crushed and heartbroken, eventually departed Sandusky and moved back to the town of Hudson, Michigan, north of Toledo, to a previous home where many of their children had been born. They hadn't lost all hope and still clung to a faith that someday they would see their precious Lillie again.

What the Bowers family didn't know was that about fifty miles west of Sandusky, near the small Ottawa County village of Genoa, on the farm of James and Jeanette Calkins, an old "gypsy" man by the name of Jack Patterson began working for them. This was about the time that Lilly had vanished in 1867. Old Jack, the gypsy, would work during the day for the Calkinses while leaving his own "tawny" children in a nearby hovel, along with a young girl of a much lighter complexion. As the story is passed down in the Calkins family records, it is noted that Mrs. Calkins had to rescue the girl from being abused:

> *One day Mrs. Calkins hearing screams rushed into the hut and rescued Lilly from the stove where she had been placed by the other children because she had refused to do their bidding. Soon after this, old Jack brought the child to Mrs. Calkins' home. She was clothed in nothing but an old coffee-sac. The Calkins adopted the child. She was given the name "Ida Bell."*

For the next fifteen years, Ida Bell Calkins was raised as their own child, although her new parents, James and Jennette Calkins, always told her they were not her real parents and that perhaps someday she might find her real family, whoever and wherever they might be.

In the years that followed, Ida Bell Calkins grew up in rural Genoa and lived with her new parents and her five stepbrothers on their eighty-acre farm near the current intersection of State Route 51 and State Route 163. Because she was so young—probably about three years old—when she was abducted, she had no recollection of her own family or her name. Despite ads and stories placed in many newspapers across the country, the Calkins family never saw the stories about the missing girl from Sandusky.

In the next fifteen years, "Ida Bell" grew to be a beautiful young woman. She had been schooled and raised to be a proper young churchgoing lady and traveled in "prominent circles" of friends. But Ida still wondered about

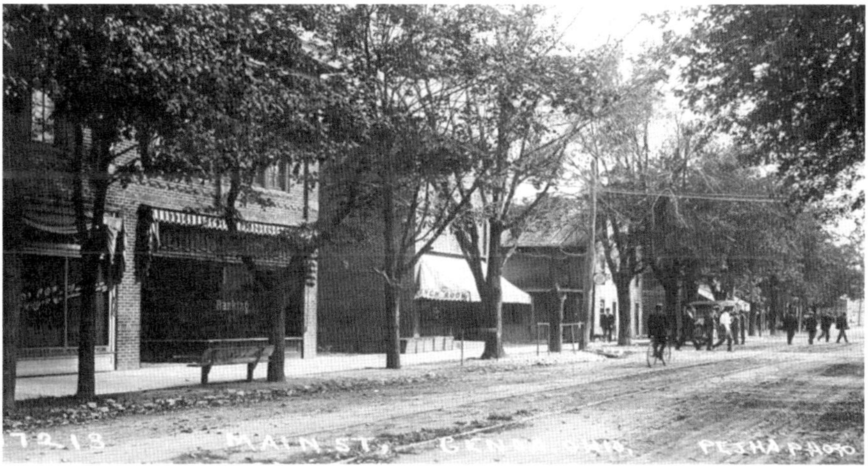

Downtown Genoa, Ohio, around 1900. *Author's collection.*

her real identity and who her parents were. Strangely, she always favored the name Lillie and wished that it had been hers. She loved the name so much that she often gave her pets that name.

In 1882, after graduation from school, she was about to be married and assume a new married name; little did she suspect that she was about to learn her real maiden name. The *Gibsonburg Christian Monthly* of July 1910 wrote that Lillie's real mother, Martha Bowers, was still living in Hudson, Michigan, and "never ceased to have faith that some day, somehow, God only knew when or how, Lillie would be restored to them."

Then, seemingly out of the blue, Mrs. Bowers received word from an old friend in Sandusky that they had heard of a young woman in Genoa who might be the long-lost Lillie. Quickly, letters were exchanged with the Calkins family in Genoa, and Mrs. Bowers soon made the trip south to Ohio to test another moment of truth. It was arranged that during a July picnic at the old GAR Hall in Genoa (which still exists), Mrs. Bower was to look at a group of girls to see if she could identify her daughter. When she saw "Ida Bell," she is said to have immediately picked her out as her daughter. There was no reunion that day, however, for Mrs. Bowers was to visit the Calkinses' home the next day to reveal herself to the girl and to see if the girl could identify her. The entire Calkins family was waiting in the sitting room when Mrs. Bowers was brought into the room. The recognition from Lillie was immediate.

"My mother," said the stunned girl. These were the first words Mrs. Bowers had heard her daughter utter since she was a toddler. Further identification

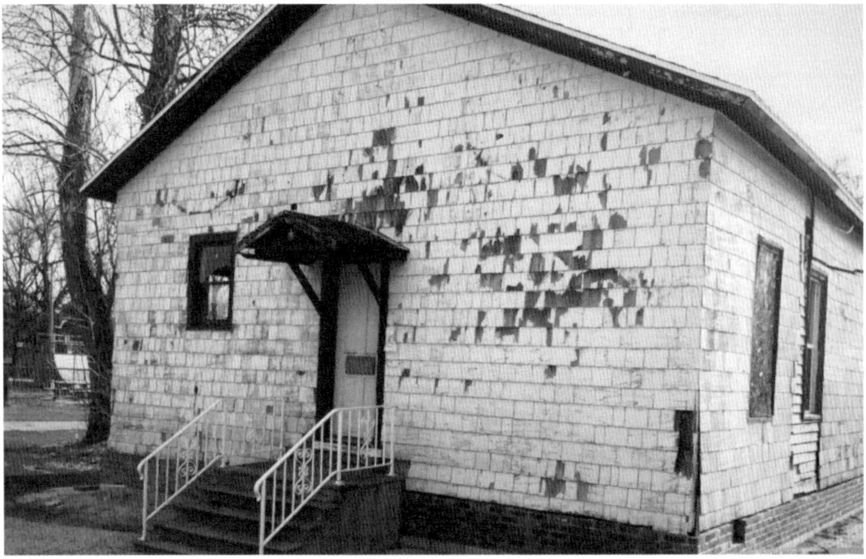

The Genoa GAR Hall where Lillie's mother first saw her long-lost daughter. *Author's collection.*

was verified by a birthmark on Lillie's head, and as Jeanette Calkins would later write, "there was joy and weeping." It was a miraculous mother-and-child reunion. After fifteen long years, the misery and mystery were over. Preparations were made at once for Marie Lillie Bowers to return to the family home in Hudson. Newspapers across the country began picking up the miracle story that had taken place in Genoa, Ohio.

Lillie was not ready to abandon her adopted home or her husband-to-be. Within weeks after the reunion, Ida Bell, or Marie Lillie, headed back to Genoa to marry a local man by the name of Daniel Cunningham. The Calkins and Bowers families seemed to have forged a strong bond. Within months, Lillie's biological baby sister, Edith Clara Bowers, would also move from Hudson, Michigan, to Genoa to marry James Levi Calkins, Lillie's stepbrother, with whom she had been raised. Both sisters remained in the vicinity until their deaths many years later. Lillie (Ida Bell) and Daniel, an oilfield worker, eventually relocated to Gibsonburg, where they raised two children. Lillie would later tell newspaper reporters that she felt very fortunate having two caring sets of parents. While she was very happy to have reunited with her real parents, the Bowerses, she held the "highest and tenderest" regard for the James Calkins family of Genoa and could not ever think of moving away from them and deserting them in their old age. Marie

Lillie "Ida Bell" Calkins-Cunningham lived in nearby Gibsonburg until she passed away at the early age of forty-five, in 1910, from a mastoid infection. She is buried at Gibsonburg along with her two children and husband—the end of a quiet story of strong faith, a mother's love and big news.

And here is how the newspapers at the time told the story.

> *Toledo, O July 27th. There was in this city today Mrs. JJ Bowers with her daughter Lillie, age 18. who had just been restored to her parents whom she had not seen for over 15 years. She had been stolen by gypsies. The family now live in Hudson Michigan and the mother and daughter were on their way home. At the time of the abduction the family lived in Sandusky. A search that extended for years failed to disclose any clew to the lost child. A few days ago a lady living near Genoa who had at one time lived in Sandusky and knew the circumstances connected with the abduction wrote to Mrs. Bowers that she believed she had a clew to their missing daughter and that she was living with a well-to-do family in that neighborhood. Mrs. Bowers went to Genoa and learned that about 14 years ago, local authorities had discovered a child in the possession of a band of roving gypsies. Feeling satisfied it was not their own, took it from them. It was then bound out to James Calkins, a farmer living near Genoa. In his family she has remained ever since, receiving the best of care and attention. The young lady is rather above the medium height, attractive and lady-like in manner and an intelligent talker.*

Chapter 14

The Last Flight of Fremont's "Million Miler"

In August 2009, an amazing discovery was announced. In the waters of the Gulf of St. Lawrence at Quebec, Canada, in a remote area of Longue-Pointe-de-Mingan, Canadian officials sent a miniature submarine equipped with cameras and lights to examine the crash site of a U.S. military seaplane that crashed in November 1942 during World War II. The Canadian teams reported back that they were able to get good sonar images and other photos of the wreckage, and the aircraft appeared to be in one piece. Not only were they able to get images of the plane, but divers were also able to reach the remote site and retrieve the remains of those Americans who went down with the aircraft when it crashed and sank. One of the bodies recovered was that of Harry "Jack" Zimmerman of Fremont, Ohio.

The tragedy occurred on November 2, 1942, as Lieutenant Jack Zimmerman and his crew were piloting a military amphibious seaplane as it attempted a take-off on the waters of the Gulf of St. Lawrence in Canada. The day was cold and the sea was rough, with swells as high as six feet. The seaplane was taking on water in its wheel wells. Despite the pilot's best effort to keep it upright, the aircraft capsized, trapping and drowning Zimmerman and his crew of four. Four others in the aircraft managed to escape and be rescued.

The discovery of the PBY-5A Catalina aircraft in 2009 was a breakthrough. For many years, it was known that the ill-fated amphibious craft was hiding somewhere in those waters, but previous efforts to find it had been

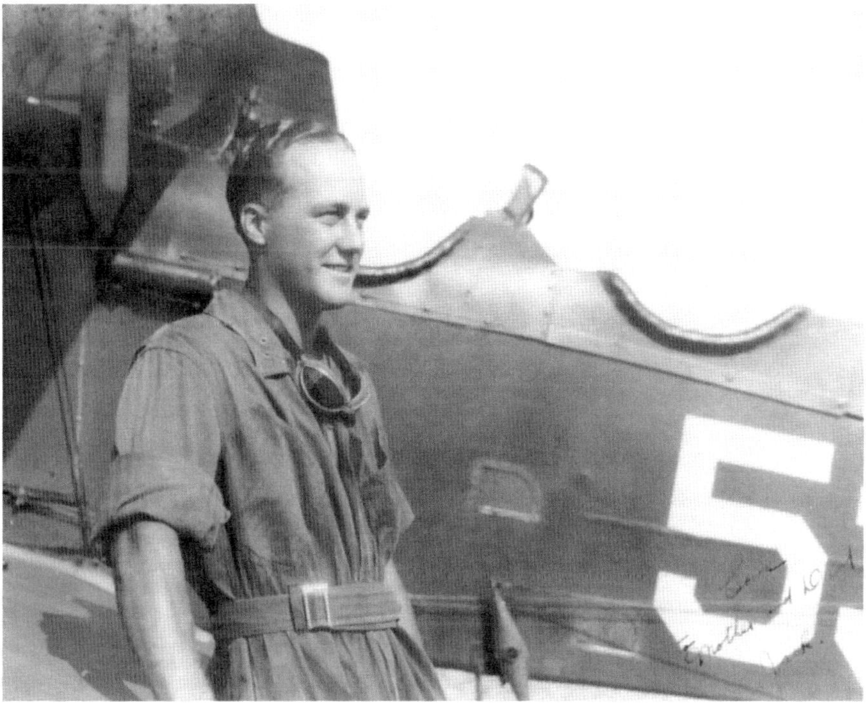

Jack Zimmerman as a young cadet pilot in training in 1928 at the age of twenty-three. *Courtesy Hayes Library and Museum.*

unsuccessful. This discovery by Canadian researchers gave new hope that perhaps this decades-old mystery would be solved and the memory of the crew laid to rest. The loss of the pilot, Jack Zimmerman, had also taken on special gravity and meaning because Zimmerman was not just any pilot. He was without doubt the most experienced pilot and one of the most famous airmen in the U.S. military, with two million miles and fifteen thousand hours logged in the cockpit flying around the world.

Harry Jack Zimmerman was born on June 6, 1906, in Fremont to his father, Harry, a leader in Fremont's well-known cutlery industry. Jack had no interest in knives but had an interest in flying from an early age. After completing high school in Fremont, he attended the Culver Military Academy and then enrolled at Dartmouth College. Soon after graduation from Dartmouth, Jack joined the U.S. Army Air Corps for training in 1928 at March Field in Riverside, California. He was put through the many paces of becoming an aviator: ground school, weather instruction, Morse code, map reading and parachute training. Finally, after many hours

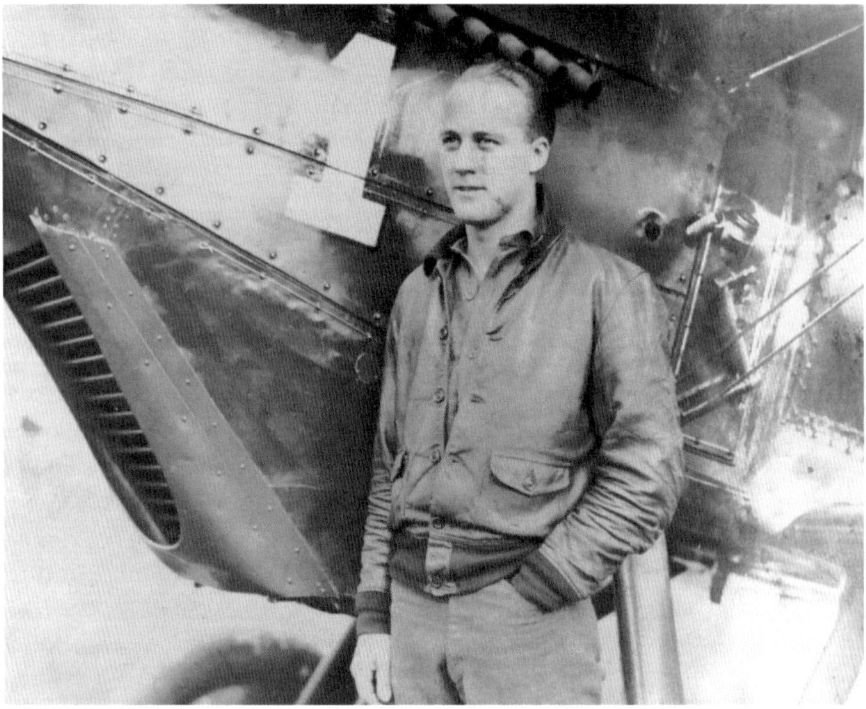

Jack Zimmerman learned to fly in the U.S. Army Air Corps in the 1920s. *Courtesy Hayes Library and Museum.*

of training with an instructor in the cockpit, he was ready to solo. His instructor said to him, "Well, Zimmerman, are you ready to take her up alone without killing yourself?" Zimmerman replied in the affirmative, and on that day, he made not just a successful take-off but a successful landing as well, and Jack Zimmerman, a twenty-two-year-old from Fremont, was reborn—as a pilot.

In 1929, Zimmerman began working for Transcontinental Air Transport behind the stick of the popular Ford Tri-Motor known as the *Tin Goose*. In 1930, Transcontinental merged with Western Air, forming what would become the airline giant TransWorld Airline or TWA. Besides passenger flights, TWA was contracted to fly the U.S. mail. Thus, Zimmerman's first years at the airlines were spent hauling the U.S. mail from city to city, putting in long hours crossing the country coast to coast.

In the only serious crash of his career while flying the mails, he was on a run from Newark, New Jersey, to Columbus, Ohio, and had to make a stop at Pittsburgh. It was December 28, 1933, and Jack says after he took

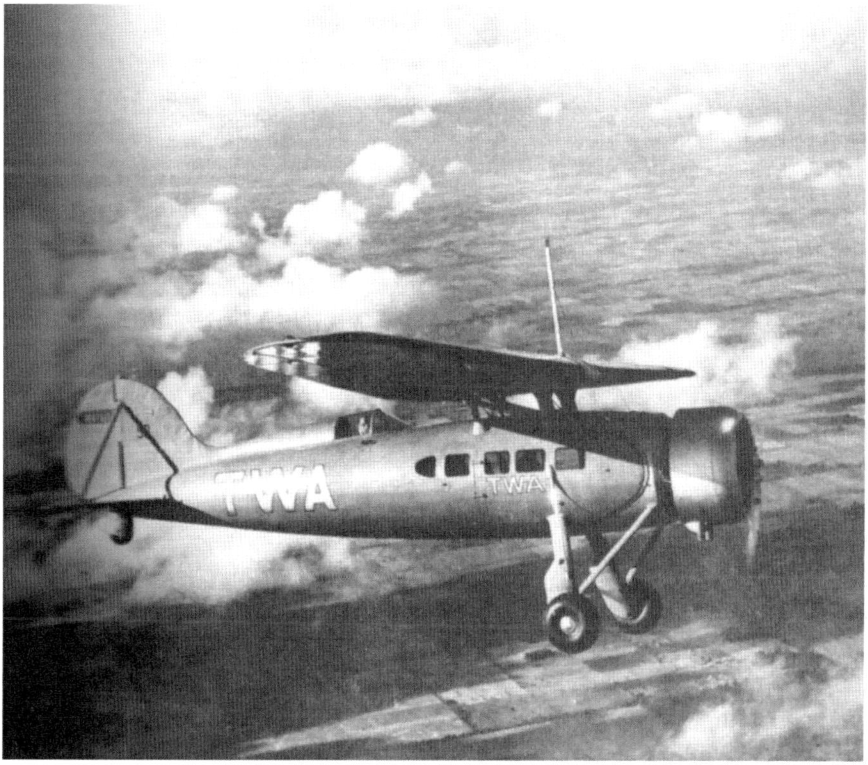

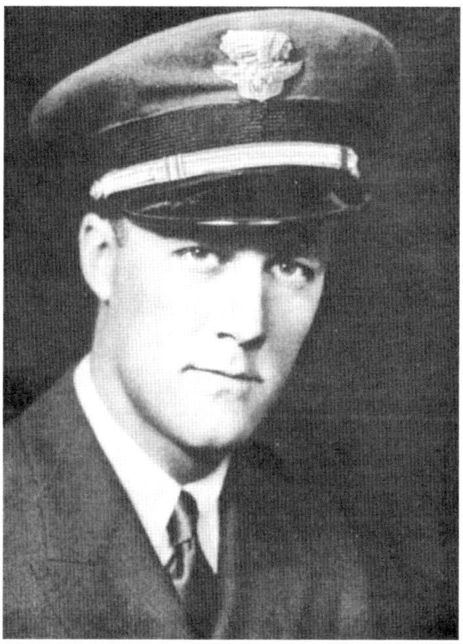

Above: Jack Zimmerman flying an early Fleetster single-engine TWA passenger plane. *TWA publicity photo in* The Million Miler.

Left: Captain Zimmerman logged more than two million miles in the cockpit and became TWA's chief pilot before returning to military duty in World War I. *From* The Million Miler.

off from the hilltop Allegheny County Airport in his Northrup Alpha, he was aloft about 150 feet when for some reason the engines quit. He had no power, and with the nearby hilly terrain, there was no room and no time to glide to safety. The plane went down fast, and he crashed into a hillside. The impact knocked him unconscious, and he was unable to move in the tangle of steel. Luckily, some witnesses ran to the scene and were able to get to Jack and pull him away from the wreckage just minutes before it exploded into a sheet of flame. Zimmerman was lucky. He survived the nightmare and was able to continue his life with his new bride, Mary Jane, and continue his profession and passion for flying.

May 1, 1936, was another night of heart-pounding excitement and one that he liked to talk about. It was not a crash or a close call but a secret assignment. He was ordered by TWA to fly to New Orleans and pick up some secret passengers under the cover of darkness. It was called Flight 7, and Captain Zimmerman recalls that after several stops en route to New Orleans, picking up some VIPs, they finally got to the Crescent City and picked up the rest of the group. By the time they departed New Orleans, there were fourteen men aboard. One of them was FBI director J. Edgar Hoover. With him was a small army of heavily armed G-men guarding their prisoner, the one and only Alvin Karpis, Public Enemy No. 1. He had just been captured and arrested that night after years on the run, and the feds were transporting "Creepy" Karpis" to St. Paul, Minnesota, to stand trial on kidnapping charges.

It was a long night and a highly secretive and circuitous trip, but Zimmerman received special written praise for his professionalism from FBI chief Hoover. It said, in part:

> *I just want you to know how much I appreciated your helpfulness on the recent special flight taken by representatives in the Karpis matter. I also wanted to compliment you on the manner with which you and Mr. Smith, the co-pilot, handled all the arrangements in connection with the flight....*
>
> *With kind personal regards, Sincerely Yours, J. Edgar Hoover.*

Zimmerman cherished the letter; it was one of the high points of his flying career. Zimmerman would have other moments in the spotlight. In 1939, he flew the last leg of the west–east inaugural record flight of TWA's first Boeing 307, known as the Stratoliner. The Boeing Model 307 Stratoliner was the first commercial transport aircraft with a pressurized cabin. Later that year, he became the first pilot to land a commercial airliner on the freshly opened runway of the new LaGuardia Airport in Queens, New York. Mayor Fiorello LaGuardia himself was there to greet the plane.

The good-looking Zimmerman was becoming a celebrity of sorts. Dubbed "Aviation's Gift to Women," he often appeared in promotions for the airlines. He was also moving his way up in the TWA ranks, not only becoming the chief pilot but also scoring the honor of having flown more than one million miles. He was a "Million Miler," the first in the nation, and he quickly evolved into a sort of poster boy for TWA. He would also become the main character of a book by popular sportswriter John Tunis. The book, *The Million Miler: The Story of an Air Pilot*, was a mix of Jack's biography and photos and a naked promotion for TWA. This book could inspire other young men to become pilots and inspire more people to fly, knowing that their planes were being piloted by smart, young and talented men like the handsome Captain Jack Zimmerman.

Reality and publishing are often full of ironies. The book was published in 1942, the same year that Jack left TWA for a while to join the war effort as World War II heated up with American involvement. The Fremont native, Zimmerman reentered the United States Army Air Corps, with which he had trained as a cadet at March Field in Riverside, California, back in 1928.

Army Lieutenant Zimmerman had been assigned to a special air group based in Presque Isle, Maine, to support the establishment of a chain of airfields in northern Canada, Greenland and Iceland. It was to be a strategic air corridor to Europe to fly aircraft and supplies to the United Kingdom from the eastern United States. The PBY-5As they were using that day ferried men and equipment to the airfield at Longue-Pointe-de-Mingan in Canada. They had completed their mission and were on their return flight to their base in Maine when on that blustery November day in 1942, the pilot's dark nemesis of bad weather came to visit. The waters were being churned viciously by the wind, and on their take-off, the seaplane was taking on too much water, coming in through the wheel wells. The plane was lurching out of control, and despite Zimmerman's best efforts to throttle back the power, hoping he could somehow regain control of the craft, it was too late. The hellish wave action of the water was getting worse, and the PBY-5A capsized. Five of the men never had a chance. They were trapped and drowning. Jack Zimmerman and his crew of four would not make it out alive. Four others in the aircraft managed to loosen themselves from the sinking craft and make it into the icy water, where they were rescued by local Canadian villagers who witnessed the tragic accident.

The world of aviation was shocked to learn of the death of Lieutenant Zimmerman. He was a well-regarded aviator who had become a friend and inspiration to many. In Fremont, his hometown, the townspeople honored their hero with a military tribute shortly after he was killed. In attendance were his parents; his sister, Mrs. L.K. Carroll of Fremont; and his wife of eleven years, Mary Jane, whom he wed in 1931.

For the next sixty-seven years, like a boat wreck, the Catalina PBY-5A lay in a watery grave, the remains of those trapped in the crash entombed in the wreckage. But then in 2009, underwater archaeologists from Parks, Canada, found the fuselage of the aircraft while conducting work in an area adjacent to the Mingan Archipelago National Park Reserve. They made the announcement, and it received considerable press coverage. For the first time in many years, the story of Jack Zimmerman's life was retold. It would take three more years, however, for the United States to act on it, sending a fifty-person team in 2012 to travel to the site to retrieve personal artifacts and remains. The team returned the airmen's personal belongings to their families. The drowned airplane still remains in the St. Lawrence waters. The bodies of the men who were lost have since been recovered, and Fremont's Jack Zimmerman is now buried at Fort Sam Houston National Cemetery in San Antonio, Texas.

In 2017, on the seventy-fifth anniversary of the crash, U.S. consul general Allison Areias Vogel unveiled a plaque to commemorate the plane crash in Québec. It was also announced that some of the artifacts found at the crash site by the nearby townspeople, including a logbook and a life vest, are currently displayed at the museum founded in the town of Longue-Pointe-de-Mingan to honor the victims. It was the brave townspeople of the village who jumped into the perilous waters back in 1942 to rescue the four survivors of the crash. To honor the U.S. servicemen who died in the accident, their names have been placed in a bronze plaque on the banks of the river near the crash site.

Private Erwin G. Austin
Private Paul D. Couzins
Captain Carney L. Dowlen
Sergeant Charles O. Richardson
Lieutenant Colonel Harry J. Zimmerman

Chapter 15

More Than Just a Drugstore

In the 500 block of Indiana Avenue sat a drugstore at the corner of City Park. It was a presence there for many years and was more than a drugstore; it became a state of mind and the heart of a neighborhood. It was Stewart's drugstore, dispensing more than just prescription drugs and patent medicines. It offered the people who lived nearby a place to have a soda, buy a magazine or candy or just gather with other folks in this predominantly African American neighborhood of Toledo called Pinewood. It was owned and run by Ella P. Stewart. She was a pharmacist who moved to Toledo with her husband, Doc Stewart, also a pharmacist, when they learned that Toledo did not have any pharmacies owned by people of color. So in 1922, Ella Stewart and Doc opened Stewart's pharmacy and soon become a part of the community. Little did she know that someday she would be honored by it, and the community would be honored to have Ella P. Stewart as a part of it. You see, Ella P. Stewart was not only a pharmacist with a friendly smile; she was also one of the first female African American pharmacists in the nation, and this extraordinary woman would also be honored as a national leader in civil rights and humanities.

Ella Stewart was born in 1893 as Ella Nora Phillips in the little community of Stringtown, West Virginia, right across the state line with Virginia. She was the daughter of poor sharecroppers and wanted to do something more with her life than remain in the grip of poverty. She attended public school in Virginia and later at Harper's, West Virginia. She excelled as an outstanding

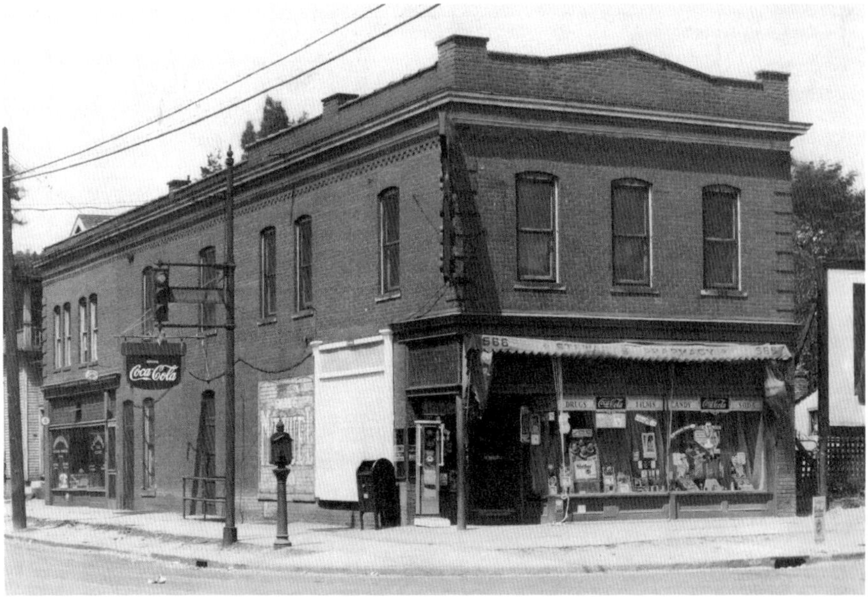

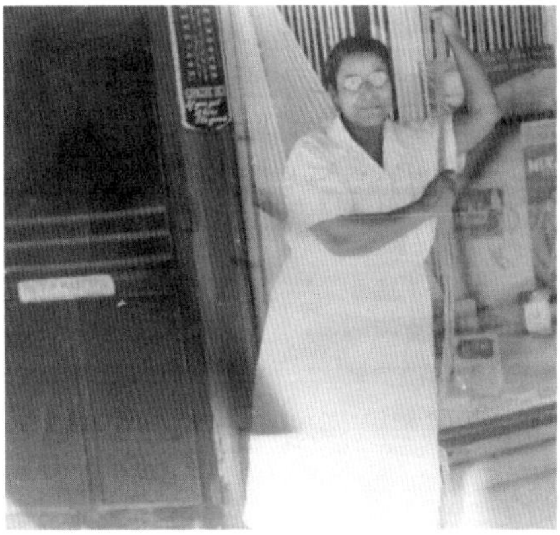

Above: The popular Stewart drugstore at Indiana Avemue and City Park in Toledo. *Courtesy Ward Canaday Collections, University of Toledo.*

Left: Ella Stewart in front of her pharmacy on Indiana Avenue. *Courtesy Ward Canaday Collections, University of Toledo.*

student, for hers was a brilliant mind, and her steel-willed determination to succeed was equally superior.

She originally sought to be a teacher, but life and times often change. An early marriage altered her plans, and she withdrew from college for a while. She became pregnant and had a child, but the promise of a life together with the child was snuffed out when whooping cough snatched the baby from her arms. Ella was not going to let tragedy defeat her. She began working again, this time in a pharmacy in Pittsburgh. She was their bookkeeper but soon developed an interest in pharmacology itself and wanted to go back to school to become a pharmacist. By 1914, Stewart had returned to the comfort of the classroom in the University of Pittsburgh's School of Pharmacy, despite being turned down several times because of racial discrimination. She persisted and wouldn't give up and finally was admitted. She was the only black female in her class. Two years later, this intelligent and ambitious young woman graduated with the highest marks in the class, becoming the first African American woman in the United States licensed to practice pharmacy. The first years after school, though, were unsettling. Ella tried opening a couple of pharmacies of her own, and eventually her early marriage ended in divorce. By 1920, she had remarried a fellow alumnus from Pittsburgh, William "Doc" Stewart. They, too, tried to carve out a life in several cities, including Detroit. It was while living in that city that they learned of the opportunity in Toledo, a city fifty miles south that was in need of a drugstore in its steadily growing African American community, the result of a great migration, as more people from the South began moving northward to get jobs in the auto industry.

Her years running the corner drugstore in Toledo were remarkable in and of themselves, as she and Doc became active members and role models in the area, especially for young people. She would frequently sit down with the children in the store to listen to their problems and offer advice. Mrs. Stewart gave out more than pills. Ella and Doc's store also was a frequent meeting place for leaders of the African American community, while Ella herself became a force of nature in her efforts to improve the overall lives of the families of color in the city. The pharmacy often hosted distinguished visitors, including luminaries such as singer Marian Anderson and W.E.B. Du Bois.

Ella P. Stewart's energy and sense of purpose put her name on a long list of organizations that she helped guide, such as the Enterprise Charity Club, the YWCA and the National Association of Colored Women (NACW). In fact, after leaving the pharmacy in the mid-1940s, she served as president of the NACW from 1948 until 1952. There seemed to be no end to her spirit of involvement and leadership on both the local and national stages—and even the world stage. In 1963, Stewart was appointed commissioner to the United Nations Education Scientific and Cultural Organization (UNESCO)—no small achievement for a woman who grew up a sharecropper's daughter in West Virginia. In addition, Stewart also created a Toledo chapter of the Pan-Pacific and Southeast Asia Women's Association (PPSEAWA). She served from 1960 to 1962 and traveled around the globe on goodwill missions, getting to meet heads of state in many nations. She was made the international vice president for the group from 1961 to 1964.

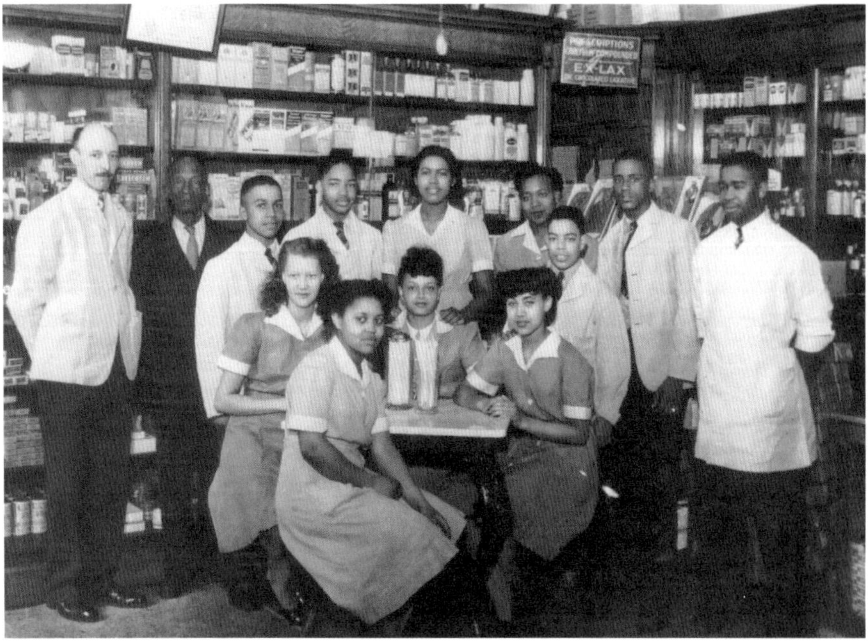

Ella and staff inside the Stewart drugstore in Toledo. *Courtesy Ward Canaday Collections, University of Toledo.*

Stewart's leadership did not go unnoticed. In 1978, she was inducted into the Ohio Women's Hall of Fame and was also honored by having an elementary school in Toledo named for her: the Ella P. Stewart Elementary School, which would later become the Stewart Academy for girls and now houses an Ella Stewart Museum. In short, Ella P. Stewart fought her entire life against the barriers of racism and triumphed over them with great dignity and an effortless grace.

Another honor awarded Stewart happened in 1957 and was the result of overt discrimination by leaders of the state of Virginia. They were inviting special guests to a big dinner to commemorate the 350th anniversary of the settlement at Jamestown. Ella received an invitation as a distinguished Virginian because she had attended school in Berryville, Virginia, as a young girl. But the invitation was rescinded when the leaders of the Virginia Chamber of Commerce learned that Ella was an African American. The unflappable Ella said she was still going to go and would RSVP. It set off a firestorm, and a national fiasco ensued as Virginia leaders tried to rescind the invitation, saying it was "all a mistake." Toledo's leaders were appalled at this blatant racism. They wanted to let Ella know that her home in

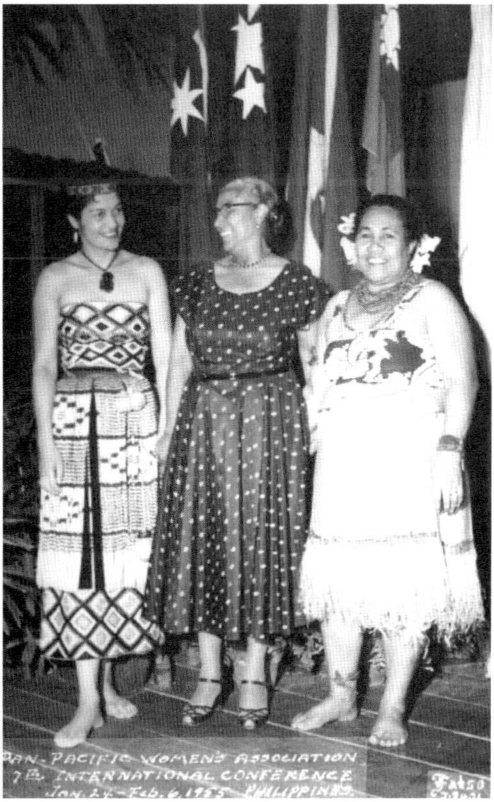

Ella Stewart on a trip to Manila in 1955 as part of a world cooperation summit. *Courtesy Ward Canaday Collections, University of Toledo.*

Toledo valued her contributions. So on the very same night of the Virginia celebration, three hundred city and church leaders in Toledo turned out to honor Ella Stewart in her hometown. The dinner was held at the Epworth Methodist Church, and Vice Mayor Ned Skeldon was one of many to speak and express their gratitude for Ella's contributions to the city: "You are everything we want in this town and we hope you stay forever." Ella called it a "crowning point in her life."

Ella would receive many more accolades in years to come, including an honorary doctorate by the University of Toledo in 1974 and a posthumous induction into the Toledo Civic Hall of Fame in 1999.

Sadly, her husband, "Doc" Stewart, passed away in 1976 after more than fifty years of marriage together. Ella later moved into a retirement community in 1980 and never let her advanced age slow her pursuit of justice for everyone. She continued working until death took her from us in 1987 at the age of ninety-four. But what death could not take from Toledo or the nation were the doors and the minds she opened for so many.

Chapter 16

Laddie Boy

A Toledo Gift to the Nation

There have been many "first dogs" that have wandered the hallways of the White House over the years, but you may not know that the first "first dog" to garner regular newspaper coverage in the United State was from Toledo. It was during the administration of President Warren G. Harding of Ohio. In March 1921, the Hardings received as an inauguration gift a seven-month-old Airedale from Charles Quetschke, an avid Harding supporter in Toledo. The popular senator from Ohio had just won the presidency in November with an impressive 60 percent of the vote and had promised a more informal atmosphere and lifestyle in the White House. The dog would help create that perception. His name was Laddie Boy, and the Hardings, with no child of their own, began to treat this lovable Airedale like a member of the family.

Both President Harding and his wife, Florence, shared a love of animals. The first lady, an advocate for the care of neglected animals, often used this handsome dog as a poster child for the promotion of animal rights. Such unprecedented attention soon made Laddie Boy the first presidential dog with a national identity. There had always been other dogs that called the White House their home in years before and since, but the Smithsonian writes that no dog has ever garnered as much publicity and press as did this dog from Toledo. He was so esteemed that he was even allowed to attend meetings with the president and other officials and was given his own hand-carved custom chair for cabinet meetings. He was no stranger to the Oval Office. A *New York Times* reporter wrote, "With many manifestations

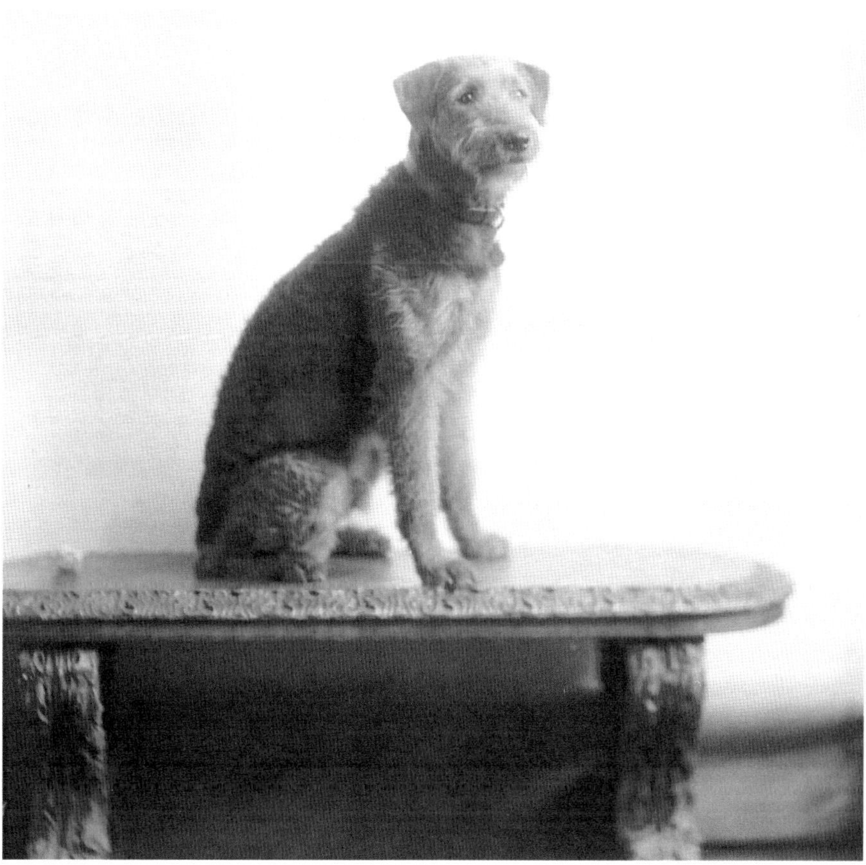

Laddie Boy was a gift to President Harding from Caswell Kennels of Toledo. *Library of Congress.*

of pleasure, the President led his new pet into his office, where he made himself at home."

Laddie Boy would rarely see the White House kennels during his tenure there, for the Airedale was frequently busy roaming the White House living quarters, endearing himself to everyone he encountered. President Harding himself would take the time to write letters to children on Laddie's behalf. Sometimes he would write letters to the press pretending to be Laddie Boy, or reporters would stage interviews with the dog. The president was so enamored with Laddie Boy that he had one thousand bronze miniature statuettes made in the dog's image shortly after taking office. He sent them to his political supporters in Washington, D.C., and Ohio. They are quite rare today and can fetch a price up to $2,000.

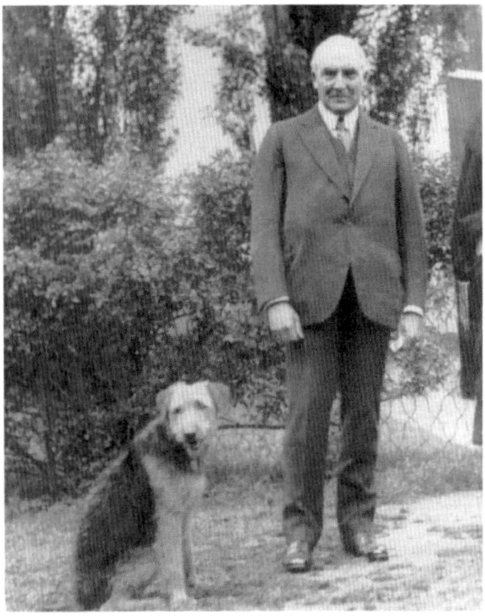

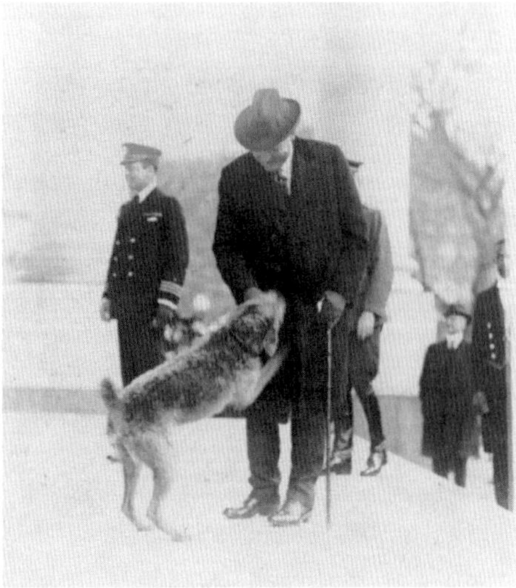

Left: Laddie Boy with his master, President Harding. *Right*: Laddie Boy greeting the president arriving home from a trip. *Library of Congress*.

Within months, this young pooch from Toledo captured the nation's heart and was elevated to be the most celebrated dog in the nation. Children nationwide loved to hear about Laddie Boy and see his pictures or get to see him in person and hug him. On July 26, each year on his birthday, he was thrown his own White House party, which other neighborhood dogs and, of course, plenty of children were invited to attend. In 1922, at his first birthday party, Laddie Boy was said to have avoided the hundreds of hands that wanted to pat him and ran away to a table apart from the crowd and just watched the children as they watched him.

It would appear that Laddie Boy was the first and only Toledoan ever to reside in the White House. Having been born at Quetschke's Caswell Kennels in Toledo in 1920, he had been sired by the internationally known Airedale champion Tintern Tip Top, also owned by Quetschke, who had gained his own interesting résumé in Toledo over the decades. He was said to have led a bit of an adventurous lifestyle over the years as a boxer, sports promoter, motorcycle racer and champion dancer. He is credited with being the man who started the Toledo Kennel Club and the Maumee River Yacht Club.

The legend and life of Laddie Boy, however, began to change when Warren Harding took ill while visiting San Francisco in August 1923. It was

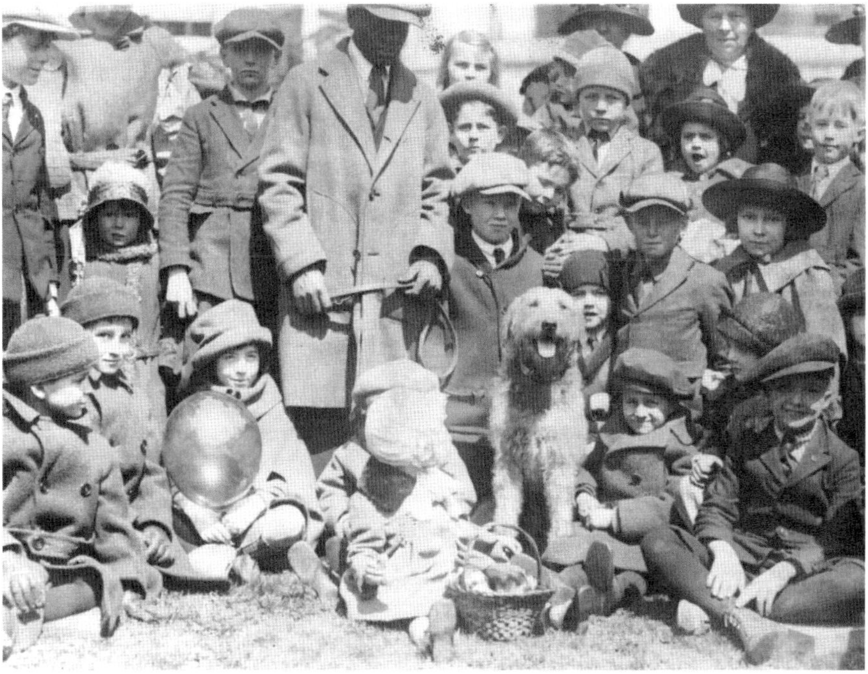

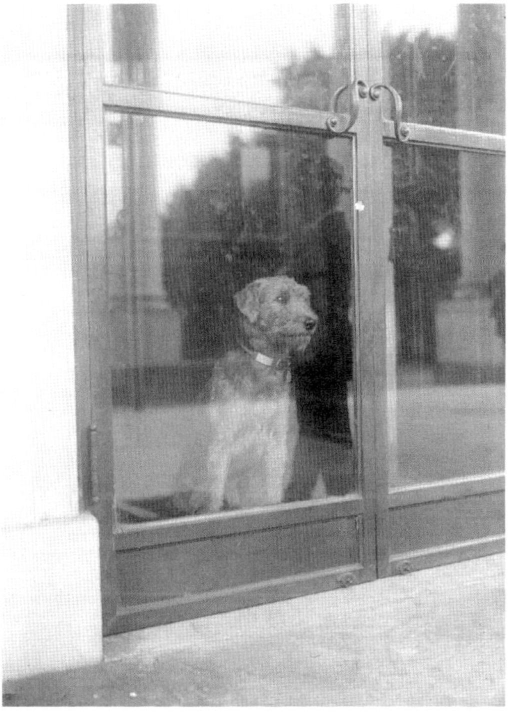

Above: Laddie Boy was a favorite with children of all ages. *Library of Congress.*

Left: Laddie Boy shown here waiting for Harding, who had suffered a fatal heart attack. *Library of Congress.*

a trip that Harding took to escape the negative attention of allegations of wrongdoing that were being lodged against him. But while in California, his heart began to fail, and Harding became gravely ill. As he lay on his deathbed, it was reported that Laddie Boy, back at the White House, could sense his master's impending death and howled constantly for three days before Harding passed away. An Associated Press reporter observed the dog's odd behavior during this somber time and wrote:

> *There was one member of the White House household today who could not quite comprehend the air of sadness which hung over the Executive Mansion. It was Laddie Boy, President Harding's Airedale friend and companion. Of late he has been casting an expectant eye and cocking a watchful ear at the motor cars which roll up on the White House drive. For, in his dog sense way, he seems to reason that an automobile took* [the Hardings] *away, so an automobile must bring them back. White House attachés shook their heads and wondered how they were going to make Laddie Boy understand.*

After the funeral for the president, when Florence Harding eventually left Washington to return home to Marion, Ohio, she gave Laddie Boy to Harry Barker, the Secret Service agent assigned to protect her. Laddie Boy would begin a new life with Barker in Massachusetts. Laddie Boy, however, did not vanish into oblivion but was recognized by thousands of newsboys around the country, who each donated a penny for a memorial to Harding and his faithful canine companion. The pennies were melted down and cast into a life-size sculpture of Laddie Boy. Today, that sculpture resides at the Smithsonian's National Museum of American History somewhere in a vault and not on public display.

In a 1992 *Toledo Blade* column, Mike Tressler wrote that when Laddie Boy was given up by Florence Harding in 1923, kennel owner Charles Quetschke of Toledo, who gave the dog to the Hardings, "begged" to have Laddie returned to Toledo, but to no avail.

Laddie Boy passed away on January 22, 1929. The *New York Times* ran a story the next day, describing the terrier as "magnificent," and reported that the "end came after the dog had been ailing for many months of old age, and died while resting his head on the arms of Mrs. Barker." Laddie Boy was buried at an undisclosed location in Newtonville, Massachusetts.

In a strange footnote to the Laddie Boy saga, in Marion at the Harding Home, a gold collar made for Laddie Boy was stolen in 2012. It was apparently

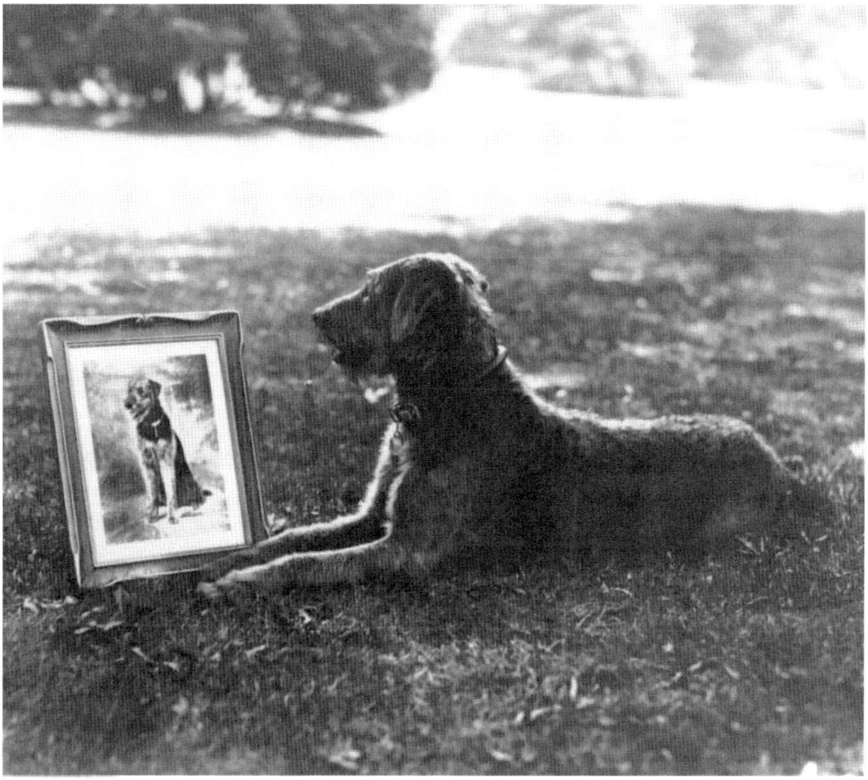

The Airedale Laddie Boy admiring his own photo on the White House lawn. *Library of Congress.*

the only item taken in a break-in at the Harding Home and Museum in Marion. A groundskeeper arrived one morning and found a ladder leaning against the home, and a second-story window had been pried open. Many of the rooms were in disarray, but nothing else was missing except the treasured gold collar. Marion police distributed photos of the collar that had been made from Alaskan gold nuggets with the name "Laddie Boy" written in raised letters on the center. So far it has not been found.

CHAPTER 17

FRANK BURT

Toledo's Greatest Showman

It was a warm spring night in May 1904 when Toledo show promoter Frank Burt starred in the biggest drama of his life on Jefferson Avenue, on the sidewalk in front of his famous vaudeville theater. He was bleeding. He had been shot in the face in a fit of anger by his wife, Addie, who was enraged that Frank was calling their marriage quits. He had told his wife earlier that morning that their marriage of seventeen years was over, so she bought a gun and some bullets at a local hardware store and went to the Burt Theater on Jefferson and Ontario, where she found Frank talking to another man out front. She tried to get him to go inside the theater, but he refused, telling her it was no use, "he was through." Then, from the folds of her dress, she drew the revolver and fired point-blank at his face, hitting him on the left side in his cheek and out through the eye socket. Seriously wounded, he grabbed his bleeding face and ran to a nearby saloon, where attempts were made to plug the gaping entrance and exit wounds. By carriage, he was rushed to nearby St. Vincent Hospital. He was in grave condition for a few days, but Frank Burt would survive and recover from his wounds. And while the marriage to Addie did not survive, Burt's marriage to his ambitions as a showman lived on for many more years and many more shows.

At the time of this violent episode in his life, Frank Burt was about forty years of age, having been born during the Civil War years in Shreveport, Louisiana. It was sugar cane country, and at a young age, Burt told the story of how he dreamed of being a duck farmer and had been promised a duck a day for every day he worked planting sugar cane. The black-eyed, shock-

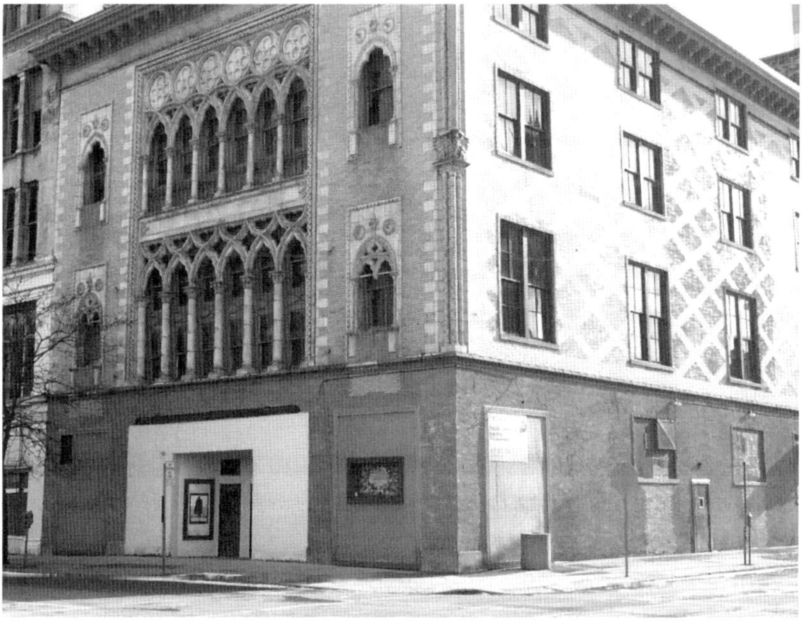

The Venetian-style Burt Theater in Jefferson Avenue in Toledo is the only remaining theater in America with Burt's name. *Author's collection.*

haired boy kept counting his ducks and was looking forward to realizing his dream when one day a group of preachers came to town and his mother, in an effort to please the men, started roasting ducks for them. Burt said he watched his duck dreams go into the oven one-by-one. It was then that Burt said he realized that he did not want to be a farmer or a tradesman. He wanted cash, not ducks, for his labor.

Burt was the son of a Confederate army officer. He was a paymaster who, according to Burt, was appointed as the superintendent of a federal prison in South Dakota after the Civil War, a job he held until his death in 1885. In that interview, Burt claimed his mother was a first cousin to Abraham Lincoln, thus helping to influence the government's decision to place a former Confederate officer in charge in a northern federal prison. At least that's the story he gave reporters about his childhood and parentage as they interviewed him upon reporting that he was opening yet another new theater in Youngstown, Ohio, in 1902. It was one of many stages the theater-man was opening throughout the nation. At the time, he was basing his management business in Toledo, where he was in charge of the Casino Dance Hall and Pavilion at Point Place, plus he had the Italianate Burt

Theater in downtown Toledo and was running the Lyceum Theater. It was also a matter of fact that Burt had an early hand in the development of Cedar Point Amusement Park at Sandusky.

So how did he get to Toledo?

In about 1887, Burt was working as a business manager for the well-known theater promoter General George Deagle. Burt says Deagle could not read or write, so Burt handled many of his contracts and other paperwork. At the same time, he was an actor's understudy to John Dillon. It was during this period that he met his wife, Addie, who was working in a vaudeville production, and it was love at first sight. They married three weeks later. They stayed on the road on the theater circuit, and then in 1893, they joined another vaudeville troupe and took a trip around the world. Burt told the reporter that when they came back to the United States, they found themselves almost penniless in New York City and ran into a theatrical manager by the name of Eddie Banks, who mentored Burt and told him to go to Toledo. He says he and his wife arrived with about $137 to their name. He took a job as the manager of the Casino at Point Place and began building his chain of theaters from that time forward. That included the building of the fifteenth-century Venetian-style building still called the Burt Theater. It was impressive, with more than 1,500 seats, and Burt even put in a "fat man's" row to accommodate the portly gentlemen of the community.

In 1900, Toledo was a growth city, and fellow businessmen were impressed with young Frank Burt. He was ambitious and creative. He brought new ideas and helped sew new life into Toledo's fabric. In 1900, for example, Burt was concerned that many of the city's poor did not have a place to get medical help or a way to get there, so he held special fundraisers at the Burt Theater to raise money for an ambulance and an emergency room where they could be taken. He also sponsored many benefits for the veterans of the city. Toledo was also impressed with the heart of the man when, in 1902, he accepted the remains of his old mentor, Eddie Banks, who had fallen on hard times and fell dead of a heart attack in Minneapolis. Burt said he'd take responsibility for the man's remains, so they were shipped back to Toledo and buried.

What most people of Toledo probably didn't know about Burt was that his real name was Frank Burton Fulenwider, not Burt. Frank's father, unimpressed with his son's flamboyant theatrical career, forbade him to besmirch the name of Fulenwider with such a scandalous vocation. So that's how Frank Fulenwider became Frank Burt—to protect the family name. As Frank's burgeoning show business empire grew across the Midwest, the Burt "brand" was becoming famous. He had a solid reputation, although it did

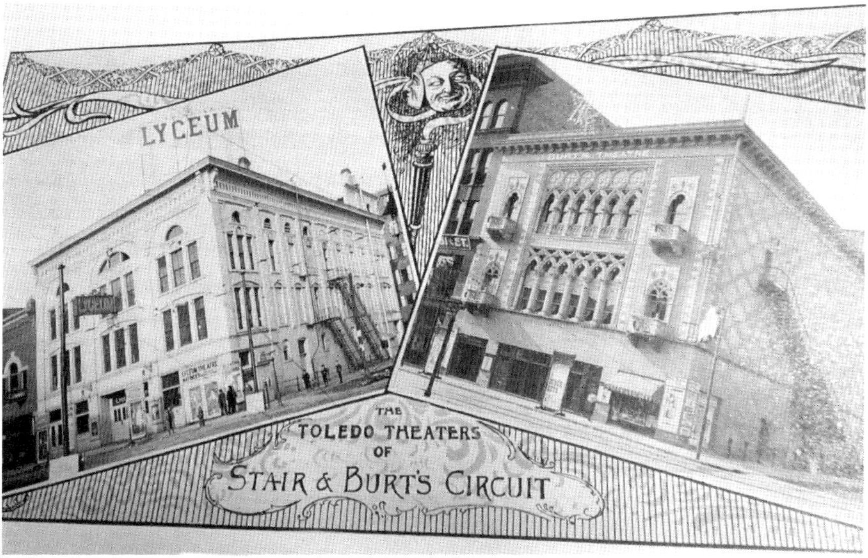

An early drawing, around 1900, of Frank Burt's theater in Toledo. *Author's collection.*

suffer a black eye in more ways than one from his wife's gunshot. She was right in her assumption that Frank was having an affair of the heart with a young performer at the theater. A few months after she shot her husband, and while she was awaiting trial for the assault, Addie Burt took ill and died. Inflammation of the brain was the official cause of death. By January, Frank Burt had quietly married Candace Morgan, a young woman about twenty years his junior, in a ceremony in Monroe, Michigan.

The new Mrs. Burt was obviously marrying a man of substance and would experience a future she could probably not yet imagine. In 1904, the ambitious Burt was already in command of theaters in Toledo, Youngstown, Fort Wayne, Akron, Cleveland, London, Ontario, Lima, Mansfield, Steubenville and Columbus, Ohio; and Evansville, Indiana. Over the next few years, he would add another two dozen theaters to the list of his holdings and would merge with even larger chains.

In 1908, Frank Burt shocked many in the theater industry when he announced that he was selling out and getting rid of all of his theaters. He was leaving the business. These were "live" theaters, after all, and perhaps he saw the threatening future of new technology of the motion picture. The film industry was just in its infancy in 1908, but it was obvious to most that films were going to be the next big entertainment thrill and would likely bring down the curtain on the era of the "live" theater.

Burt also announced that he was leaving Toledo and moving to Denver, Colorado, where the drier climate might better suit the health of his wife, Candace. And so Burt soon left the city on the Maumee behind him and headed toward the future. Not one to rest for long, in Denver, Burt was instrumental in developing Lakeside Amusement Park, a large park of Ferris wheels, roller coasters, funhouses and a glittering midway with games of chance and skill. It was not unlike Cedar Point on Lake Erie, which he had managed in its early years. Perhaps a testament to his business savvy is the fact that both Lakeside Amusement Park and Cedar Point are still in operation to this day. After his success in Denver, the next big challenge for Burt was in California, where he was named the "chief of concessions" for the Panama-Pacific Exposition of 1915. It was a moment where experience meets opportunity. With his extensive background in management, amusements and theater, he was considered the perfect choice for this most challenging of roles at the exposition. He was to manage the admissions and the Joy Zone, the primary midway of entertainment and amusement venues and rides. Burt did not disappoint. He was masterful in this role. He devised a financial scheme with the concessionaires to pay them and to take control of their operations. He also promised and delivered only "class" concessions in a beautiful setting; there were no shady dances of the day like the "Bunny Hug" or the "Grizzly Bear" and no depictions of catastrophes and so-called girlie shows. He also tried using new technologies where he could to improve the management and monitoring of the admissions. In one example, he utilized the invention of a young man in Portland, Oregon, who developed the first automatic tabulating turnstile. By using this new device, Burt was able to keep a running count of how many tickets had been sold at any time of day.

The exposition was a smashing success for San Francisco, and Burt was a key player. His legacy, though, was far from over. The community of Seal Beach in Southern California, south of Los Angeles, was impressed with Burt's success at the exposition and brought him to town to help them create the Seal Beach boardwalk and Joy Zone. As with Lakeside in Denver or dozens of other amusement parks he helped create, it appeared that Burt's touch was golden. Seal Beach became yet another enduring legacy of Burt's brilliance and showmanship. Burt was contracted for other amusement parks in other western U.S. cities, and then he decided to try yet another new career: the movies. By 1920, he was launching his own motion picture company. It was not in Hollywood but in San Mateo, near San Francisco. Burt formed Pacific Studios and tried producing movies in Northern California locations, but this time, perhaps because he didn't understand

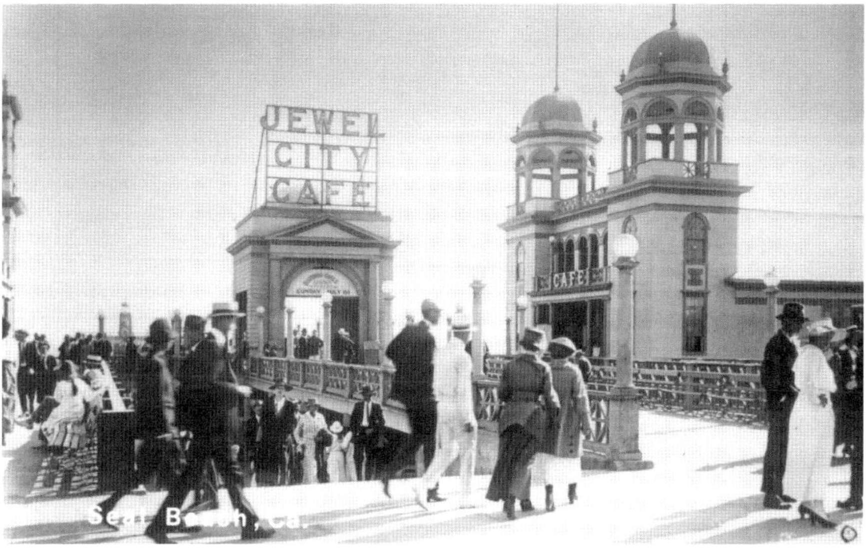

Seal Beach boardwalk in California, managed by Frank Burt about 1916. *Courtesy of City of Seal Beach, California.*

the nascent film industry that was still evolving, his efforts were frustrated. He contracted for more amusement park projects, but in 1924, the energetic Burt fell ill, and the man who helped bring joy and smiles to millions of people would bring sorrow to those who knew him. At the age of sixty-two at his home in San Mateo, Franklin Burton Fulenwider died.

He will be remembered as Frank Burt, and in Toledo, his legacy still breathes life. The Burt Theater on Jefferson endured as a venue for popular entertainment long after Burt was gone. In the 1950s, it gained local attention as the Peppermint Lounge, hosting big names in the entertainment world, and then later became the Country Palace, a country and western bar, where it was discovered to have been the "bar-room in Toledo, across the depot" in the famous Kenny Rogers hit "Lucille" in 1973. The old structure would later become Caesar's Show Bar, and on the sidewalk where Burt almost died from a gunshot wound one hundred years earlier, drag queens from across the country and their fans would gather to crowd into the Burt Theater for a night of ribald entertainment.

Today, the grand building is being refurbished in efforts to renew its Venetian architecture and elegant design of exterior brickwork. And once again, it is being called the Burt Theater. One can only think that Toledo's great showman is watching from the wings.

Chapter 18

The Cutter *Storis*

The Death of a Toledo Queen

From Jamie Farr Park on Summit Street in North Toledo, if you look across the Maumee River to the opposing bank on the east side, you can glimpse one of the oldest operating legacies of the city: the Toledo Shipyards. It is here where scores of ships, large and small, have been built and launched. For nearly 130 years, this site along the Maumee has been the cradle of creation for the maritime industry on the Great Lakes, from the production of wooden schooners and cargo ships of the nineteenth century to a fleet of giant steel lake freighters and other vessels of the twentieth.

The list of ships that have come off the docks to splash their maiden hulls into the waters of the river at this location is lengthy and impressive. There were about 180 from 1890 to 1981. Add to that the myriad ships that are also repaired in the dry docks and nearby slips every year—even to this day.

The first boat built there was in 1890, when it was the Craig Shipbuilding Company. That first vessel was a wooden schooner named the *Churchill*. It was lost in a storm in 1898 on Lake Michigan. That was not an unusual fate in the early days of shipping on the sometimes unpredictable waters of the Great Lakes. There were many ships that were birthed in Toledo only to be lost or foundered in a storm, and some were even lost in war.

The *Lake Fife*, a 250-foot steel steamer cargo ship built in Toledo in 1919, later to become an Italian flagged vessel, was torpedoed by the British warship the HMS *Unique* in 1941 off Tunisia. All twenty-eight crew members were lost. It was one of at least a half dozen vessels built in Toledo that were lost to the weapons of war. Most ships, however, are lost to the war of economics.

They get too expensive to maintain, or they are just no longer seaworthy or viable. Their fate is typically to be scrapped and sold off for salvage.

There was one ship built in Toledo that suffered this indignity of "salvage" most recently that still raises the blood pressure of those who loved it; it might be Toledo's most famous ship. It was WAG 38, the U.S. Coast Guard cutter *Storis*. Perhaps you've heard of it; perhaps not. It's quite likely you've heard of its twin, the legendary icebreaker *Mackinaw*.

In the 1940s, as Toledo's industry began the task of building the nation's tools of war during World War II, the Toledo Shipbuilding Company was given the contracts to build two Coast Guard icebreakers, similar in size and design but with different roles to play when put into service. The *Mackinaw* would be used as a giant icebreaker on the Great Lakes to keep the shipping lanes open for as long as possible during the winter months so that critical transportation of coal and other materials could flow freely between cities. It was the second one built at the shipyards and would achieve great acclaim on the Great Lakes for many decades. But the first breaker built is the one that most people in Toledo don't remember. It was called the *Eskimo*, or the *Storis*, as it would be christened later. The mission of the *Storis* would not be on the Great Lakes but would be to break ice in the North Atlantic and to

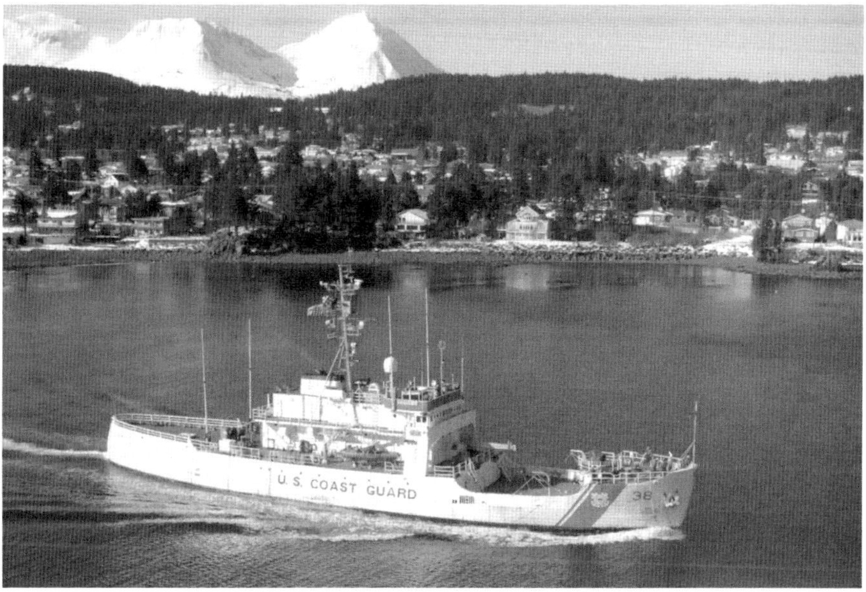

U.S. Coast Guard cutter *Storis* leaving Kodiak, Alaska, for the last time in 2007. *Photo by U.S. Coast Guard.*

open up sea lanes where military transports needed passage. The shipyard workers in Toledo were proud of their contribution to the war effort, and as more men were needed for military service, the dry docks and rivet crews at the yards were starting to be filled with men and women doing their part for Uncle Sam.

It was in this war footing atmosphere that on July 15, 1941, the keel was laid down in Toledo for a new navy cutter of 230 feet in length at a cost of $1 million. The *Toledo Blade* reported that navy representatives and shipyard executives joined hundreds of workers at the shipyards for the laying of the keel celebration. At the same time, Hitler was invading Russia, Charles Lindbergh was urging the United States to stay out of the war in Europe

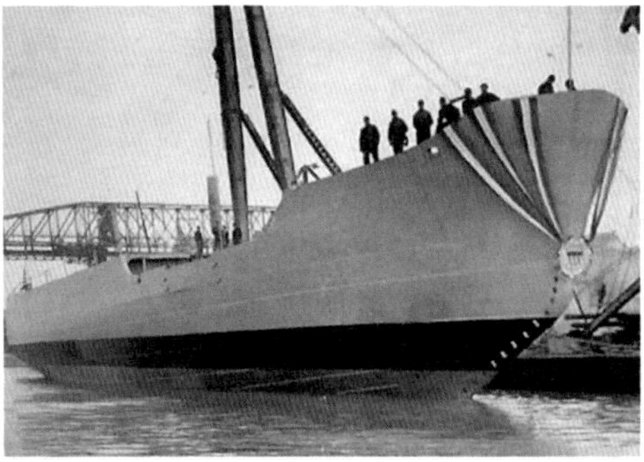

Left: The cutter *Storis* launched at Toledo, April 1942. *Photo by* Toledo Blade.

Below: Launching of Coast Guard cutter *Storis* at Toledo Shipyards, 1942. *Photo by* Toledo Blade.

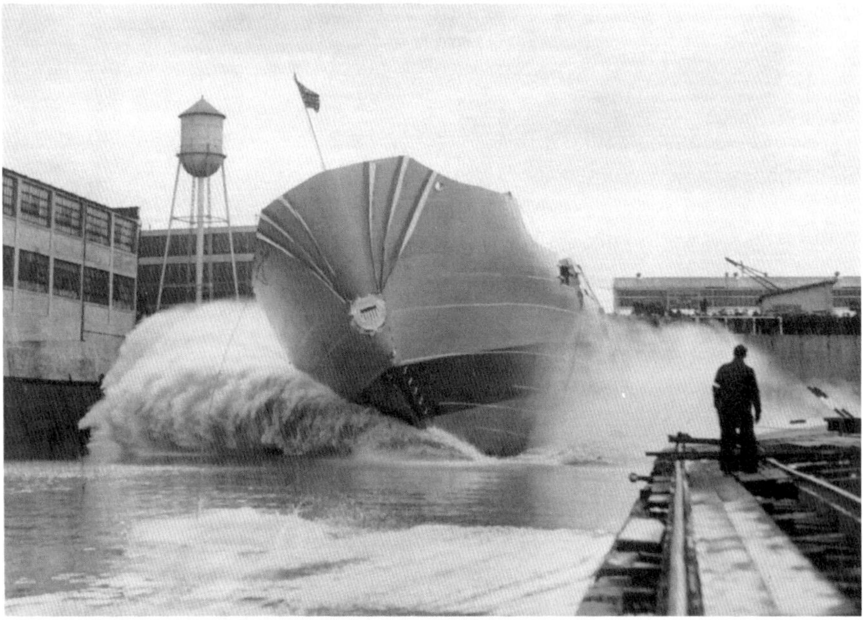

and "Chattanooga Choo-Choo" was the most popular song on the radio. In the ensuing months, the United States would no longer be preparing for war but would enter the conflict after the Japanese attack on Pearl Harbor in December. Now war production and activity would accelerate even more, and the big cutter being built in Toledo would be ready to hit the water in just nine months. On April 4, 1942, the cutter was launched as the *Storis*. It was an anglicized version of the Danish word *sirorsuit*, meaning "large ice." The original name that was to be bestowed on the cutter was "Eskimo," but because it was to be deployed for duty in the Arctic Circle, it was noted that the word "Eskimo" was considered offensive in many countries of that region, including Canada and Greenland. Thus, even in 1942, political correctness was a prudent priority, and the name *Storis* was given to the new ship.

It was an appropriate name because it meant "large ice," and that would be the target of this American icebreaker for many years. After the *Storis* was commissioned in September 1942, it was dispatched for immediate duty along the coast of Greenland as the mother ship for a fleet of patrol boats that were in the hunt for German U-boats and any attempts by the Germans to build weather or radar installations in Greenland. The *Storis* was one of only two ships that could also carry a seaplane with it to help observe from the air as well as the sea. It was part of an operation called the Greenland Patrol and was responsible for escorting ships bringing men and supplies to Greenland and sometimes for breaking a path through the ice to assist their arrival, plus finding and removing any enemy military activity. There were several other cutters also working the North Atlantic, and by the war's end, it was recorded that between July and October 1944, *Northland*, *Storis*, the *Eastwind* and *Southwind* had captured sixty Germans while destroying Axis weather stations on the northeast coast of Greenland, effectively ending Axis weather observation from Greenland.

The *Storis* would also receive commendations for its part in helping rescue sailors who were aboard the Coast Guard cutter *Escanaba*. In June 1943, while the *Storis* was helping escort a convoy to Newfoundland, the cutter *Escanaba* experienced a still mysterious on-board explosion. The *Storis* was one of two ships sent to investigate and rescue any survivors. By the time it arrived, the *Escanaba* was already under water. They found 2 survivors, but the other 103 crew members went down with the ship. It was the worst maritime disaster for the Coast Guard during World War II; ironically, the *Escanaba* had just months before rescued more than 130 survivors from the USS *Dorchester*, a passenger ship blown up by a German submarine.

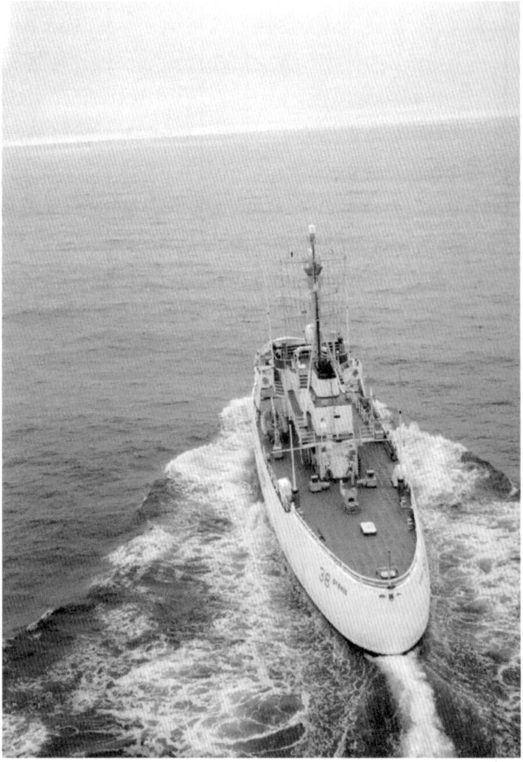

Right: *Storis* cruising in the northern Pacific. *Photo by U.S. Coast Guard.*

Below: Cutter *Storis* on cruise. *Photo by U.S. Coast Guard.*

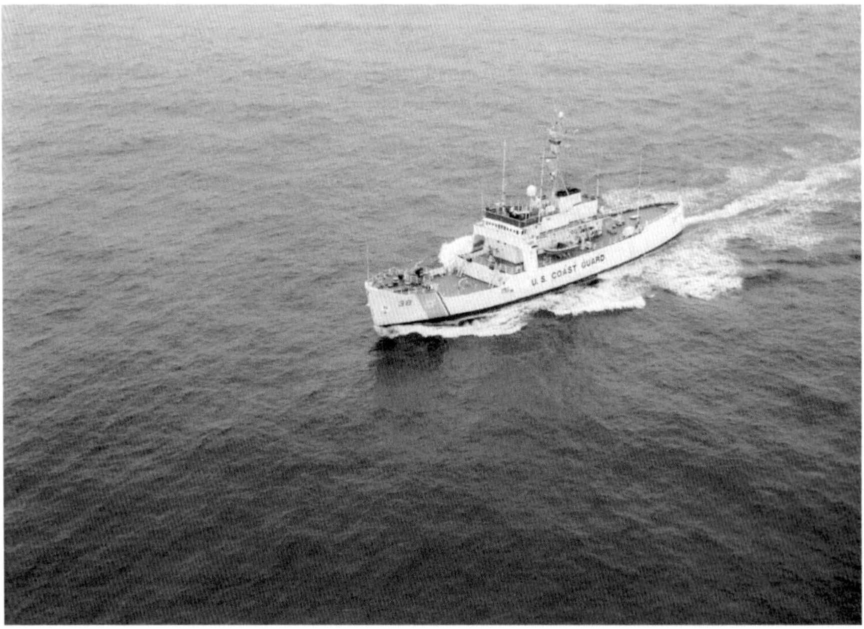

After World War II, the *Storis* stayed in the Atlantic for a few years, but by 1948, it was deployed to Juneau, Alaska. Here it was assigned to Bering Sea patrols to help move supplies and medical aid during the frozen winter months to the remote villages in the Aleutian Islands and outer regions of Alaska. It became a familiar and welcome sight to many of the Inuit peoples whose lives were made easier by the ship and crew.

In 1957, this Toledo-made ship made navigation history. In concert with the Coast Guard cutters *Bramble* and *Spar*, the trio was to search for a deep draft channel through the Arctic Ocean and to collect hydrographic information and soundings for future journeys. *Newsweek* magazine wrote in its July 15, 1957 edition:

> *The United States Coast Guard cutters STORIS, SPAR, and BRAMBLE were "bucking the broad swell" of the North Pacific this week, on their way to the Arctic and to the high adventure, their commanders hoped, of sailing across the roof of the continent to New York City. Their mission: To find an escape route for radar-line supply ships which might become trapped in the Arctic by ice.*

They eventually made it through and were the first U.S. military vessels to do so. The Canadian government even named one of the passages through the icy channels the Storis Passage. Upon its return to the waters of Greenland, the *Storis* thus became the first U.S.-registered vessel to circumnavigate the North American continent. In doing so, it earned a rightful place in the National Historic Register for that accomplishment.

The *Storis* would head for open sea again and move through the Panama Canal and back up the Pacific Ocean to the frigid waters of the Alaskan coast. Its new assignment was in Kodiak on Kodiak Island. Part of its mission was to keep in check the large fleets of Japanese and Soviet vessels that moved in to harvest the abundant stocks of crab and bottom fish in Alaskan waters. Boarding teams frequently visited these vessels to verify their catches. Although seemingly inconsequential, these vessel boardings and deceptive lighting and fishery surveillance were important to understanding the fishing fleet. During these often elusive cat-and-mouse games, the *Storis* crew would track and plot the position of these vessels and discover them hovering just outside U.S. waters. In 1967, the *Storis* crew boarded and seized a Soviet fishing vessel within a mile of the U.S. coast, resulting in a $5,000 fine, the first ever such seizure of a Soviet vessel. In 1972, the *Storis* seized two Soviet fishing trawlers, and while escorting them to port, one of them attempted to escape several times.

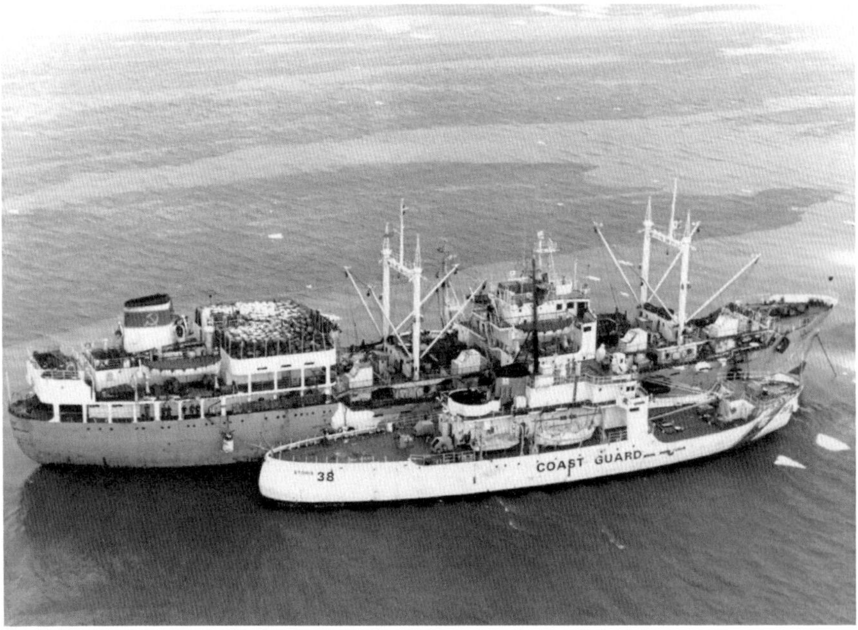

Storis coming to the rescue of a foreign tanker. *Photo by U.S. Coast Guard.*

Each time, the *Storis* would force it back on course. The *Storis* soon earned the nickname the "Galloping Ghost of the Alaskan Coasts."

It continued to serve proudly for years after and helped break ice for the Alaskan Pipeline in 1975 in Prudhoe; years later in 1989, it would help in the emergency clean-up of that Alaskan oil when the *Exxon Valdez* went aground in Prince William Sound. Finally, in 1991, when the Coast Guard cutter *FIR* was decommissioned, the *Storis* became the "Queen of the Fleet": the longest-serving cutter, with nearly fifty years of service to its country. This product of Toledo would wear the gold letters on its hull to denote its status as the "Queen." The *Storis* would enjoy another sixteen years of wearing the crown before finally, in 2007, the *Storis*, nearly sixty-five years after its hull was splashed into the waters of the Maumee River in 1942, was decommissioned.

At its decommissioning ceremonies it was noted that the *Storis* had saved 250 lives, saved 25 ships and boats, assisted more than 100,000 people in the remote villages of the Bering Sea, boarded over 7,000 vessels and traveled more than 1.5 million miles. At the ceremony in Kodiak, Rear Admiral Arthur "Gene" Brooks of the Coast Guard told the crowd:

> *Today, we bid farewell to a beloved cutter that has served her nation with legendary distinction. This "Queen" has literally carved a path, blazed the trail and marked the waterways that ensured the safe transit of every ship that followed. It's obvious; this tough old ship has the tenacity and determination—the very heart and soul—of those who built her, those members of the greatest generation. Throughout the years, the crew members at her helm have demonstrated extraordinary courage and fortitude saving lives, protecting living marine resources and protecting shipping from the hazards of the icy Arctic. For you see, while* Storis *is this hearty ship, the real* Storis *is every Coast Guard crew member, every crew, that ever sweated—and toiled—and laughed—and dreamed—aboard her. These are the lives. These are the Coast Guard heroes, who breathed life—and passion—and purpose.*

It was assumed at the 2007 decommissioning that the *Storis* would become a museum ship; because of its long service on the Alaskan coast, most likely it would find a home port in Juneau or Kodiak. But because those Alaskan communities are not large and it would be difficult to support and maintain a ship that large on visitor fees and contributions, an effort was made by a group in Toledo to bring the *Storis* "home" to Toledo, where it was built. In Toledo, it could be honored as a museum ship, a well-deserved honor after its historic contributions to the nation. But attempts as late as 2012 to pass legislation in Washington to give the cutter *Storis* to Toledo were stymied by what amounted to politics on Capitol Hill. Instead, the historic ship was placed into the General Service Administration's inventory of surplus ships to be sold to the highest bidders. It was a humiliating and frustrating turn of events, especially for the thousands of Coast Guard veterans who had served aboard the ship and knew it was special. But negotiations continued with the GSA to give the Toledo group, the Last Patrol, more time to raise the funds needed to buy and transfer the *Storis* from the "ghost fleet" of salvage ships near San Francisco back to Toledo.

Despite what the Toledo group thought was an understanding that it would get special consideration because it wanted to preserve the *Storis*, the understanding was inexplicably scuttled by the GSA, which felt it had lived up to the regulations for disposal, and then put it up for a two-week bid process. It came as a shock to the nonprofits in Alaska and Toledo that wanted to save the ship. They needed time and money and had neither. So the *Storis* sold at auction for a lone bid of $70,100, not to preservationists or the Toledo group that wanted to bring it home as a sea cadet training ship and museum but to two men who had formed a scrap metal and salvage company. Despite numerous eleventh-hour legal objections and a flurry of protests by various interest groups, the proud *Storis*, WMEC-38, the "Queen of the Fleet," which helped save many lives, was about to be put to death. In 2014, the cutter was towed from the storage area at Alameda, California, and taken to a "shipbreaking" yard in Ensenada, Mexico, where it was systematically dismantled and carved up for scrap steel. What Toledo workers had built with devotion, patriotism and pride was being savaged and plundered for a fast buck. It was an abomination, and yet, there was nothing to be done. The *Storis* is now but a memory. The only thing left to do is to tell the story of this exceptional ship and how it was built in Toledo and reigned the seas as the "Queen of the Fleet."

Chapter 19

When Toledo Was "Gangster Junction"

The afternoon of February 5, 1930, brought great excitement to the downtown streets of Sylvania. The sounds of gunshots ripped through the frigid air, and shoppers on the street scrambled for cover as a group of bandits held up the Farmers and Merchants Bank at the corner of Main and Erie. The robbers lined customers up against the wall inside the bank and, with the threat of their guns, ordered the cashiers to open the vault. The cashier locked the vault instead, and one of the bandits threw him to the ground and began beating and kicking him. The leader of the gang ordered the man to stop and to just get the cash from the bank drawers. A teller sounded an alarm, but it was too late. Within minutes, the bandits dashed out the door to get in a waiting car. E.C. Howard, a service station operator nearby, saw them and fired on them with a shotgun. He hit no one. In the end, the "yeggs" or robbers were back in their car, and with $2,000 in cash, they drove away, probably planning their next robbery.

Such crimes were not uncommon in the Midwest during this period, as roving gangs of robbers roamed the small towns of America looking for an easy haul. The Toledo area was not immune to this scourge of lawlessness and seemed to be a magnet for criminals, small-time and big-time. In the Sylvania bank robbery, it was the latter, for three months later, on May 20, two men were brought to Toledo from Akron for questioning and a lineup in connection with the bank heist. One of them gave his name as Frank Mitchell of Kansas City, although he wasn't Mr. Mitchell. His real name was Charles Arthur Floyd, who would be better known as "Pretty Boy Floyd."

"Frank Mitchell" was later tried and convicted in Lucas County in November and sentenced to twelve years in prison. An hour before sentencing though, he tried to escape from his jailers. It was short-lived. After five brief minutes of freedom, he was back in cuffs and before the bench. The story didn't even make the front page. Little did Toledo's prosecutor know he was dealing with a man who would become one of the era's deadliest gangsters and would someday be Public Enemy Number One.

The escape attempt of Floyd in Toledo should have been a warning. While on his way to Columbus to begin serving his twelve-year sentence, he escaped again, vowing never to be taken alive. He would get his wish. His reign of terror would continue for another five years and also pay a deadly revisit to northwest Ohio when, in April 1931, the escapee Pretty Boy Floyd returned and took up residence in Bowling Green with two women and a local criminal with the nickname of "Billy the Killer." They got into a shootout with the police chief and a patrolman by the name of Ralph Castner, who was mortally wounded in the exchange. He would tragically die from his wounds a week later. The police chief returned fire on the fugitives, and one of his shots found Billy the Killer and sent him sprawling to the pavement in a lifeless heap. The chief also shot one of the women, who had picked up Billy's gun. She, too, would later die. Over the next several weeks, local police were on the lookout, for it was believed that Floyd was hiding in Toledo with friends. If he was, he was never found, and Floyd would go on to murder at least four more police officers and others. Floyd's luck would run out in 1934, when he was shot to death while being pursued by G-man Melvin Purvis in East Liverpool, Ohio.

TOLEDO BECAME A CROSSROADS OF VIOLENCE

These criminal events unfolding in the Toledo area during this era were far from isolated. It was the age of prohibition, and the rival gang wars in the Midwest for control of the booze business set in motion a steady wave of violence and bloodshed. Newspapers of the day were filled with headlines of kidnappings, murder, mayhem and robberies. Toledo was no stranger to the spasms of gang violence, as the Licavoli gang from Detroit tried muscling its way into the city to take over the vice rackets and illegal booze trade. The group wasn't welcome here, and its ambitions led to the notorious killing of Toledo's young club owner and bootlegger Jack Kennedy. There were other local gangsters who left chaos in the wake of their ambitions. Toledo was also a hot spot for illegal gambling dens, and Jimmy Hayes, a Toledo kingpin of the gambling rackets, was only lucky for a while. Every hot streak cools down, and so did his body temperature when he was found dead in a Detroit alley. The names of those poor souls who were written down in the coroner's log could have filled pages through the '20s and '30s. They were both good guys and bad guys, and some of them weren't guys: Louise Bell (bootlegger Jack Kennedy's girlfriend), Jack Kennedy (bootlegger), Ralph Zahnle (dry agent), Max Gross (Toledo bootlegger), Walter Kruse (Toledo policeman), Archie Dennison (gangster), Earl Bracker (businessman), Norman Blatt (gambler), Abe Lubitsky (bootlegger), Jim Leahey (bootlegger), Sam Armetto, Ben Migura, Chester Marx (club owner), "Dago Holly" Parlow (gangster), Aaron Harris (bootlegger), Harry Gertzlein (gangster), John Incorvaia (local hoodlum), Al Jaffee (gangster), John McLaughlin (hotel clerk), Charles Ebnerr (Point Place rumrunner) and Augie Annarino (bootlegger), just to name a few. There were other bootleggers killed in shootouts with the Coast Guard on Lake Erie, and some Coast Guardsmen also lost their lives in the fight against the smugglers moving liquor and beer from Canada.

Dillinger Slept Here

While much of the violence was inspired by the brutality of the local mob wars and the profits from illegal prohibition activity, there was also a vicious subset of gangsters who were essentially freelancers who specialized in armed robbery, or working for the highest bidder. They weren't connected to the big organized crime syndicates but worked alone, roaming the country, stealing money, doing hits. The larger-than-life John Dillinger was one of them and was known to frequent northwest Ohio on occasion. He robbed a bank in Bluffton, Ohio, in 1933, and then got caught, only to shoot his way out of the Allen County Jail at Lima. It was a tragic jail escape in which Sheriff Jess Sarber was shot and killed by Dillinger's allies as they stormed the jail to set him free. In 1934, Dillinger would return to northwest Ohio. On May 3, 1934, he and his gang robbed the First National Bank in Fostoria, spraying the bank and downtown with bullets from two Tommy guns. People ran for cover, but several townspeople were wounded in the mêlée, including the police chief, and no one was killed. The robbery netted the gang about $17,000 in cash and bonds. Was Dillinger ever in Toledo? Probably. The getaway car used in the Fostoria robbery was a Ford stolen in Toledo.

EGAN'S COLD-BLOODED KILLER RATS

The Tommy gun, a fully automatic .45-caliber weapon originally designed for warfare, became the weapon of choice for most of the gangsters during the era. Until the mid-1930s, they were available and legal for purchase. They were intimidating, loud and deadly. In April 1928, an American Express mail truck carrying the New York Central payroll became the target of machine gun–wielding bandits who seized the truck and the guards in South Toledo near the train station and then took it to a hidden location, where guards were bound and gagged and the safes were removed and put into two waiting getaway cars. On Upton Avenue, near Bancroft, several miles from where the truck was captured, two Toledo police officers, George Zientara and John Biskupski, just happened to be on routine patrol when they saw the two speeding cars and watched as they pulled into the garage of an apartment house on Upton Avenue. There were no two-way radios yet in the patrol cars, and they had no idea what they were walking into. As the two officers tried to get a better view of the house, gunshots erupted, first from a rifleman in an upstairs window and then from a machine gunner who burst out of the garage. Biskupski was shot at but was not hit and returned fire; his partner, George Zientara, a twenty-eight-year-old father of four, was not as lucky. He was hit directly in the head from machine gun fire. He would die later that day at the hospital.

The five bandits had little choice but to abandon the hundreds of thousands of dollars' worth of loot they had stolen. They bolted from the garage and escaped in the police car. Police would later learn that the gang consisted of seven men, two women and two children, likely members of one of the branches of the notorious St. Louis–borne gang called Egan's Rats. They had been renting the apartment for a couple of months and probably were planning the heist and keeping watch on the movements of the payroll trucks. It was also learned or speculated later that two of the gunmen were Raymond "Craneneck" Nugent and Fred "the Killer" Burke. Their names would go down in criminal lore, as they were believed to be two of the gunmen in the bloody St. Valentine's Day Massacre in Chicago on February 14, 1929, when Al Capone hired them to gun down seven members of the Bugs Moran gang in a bloody struggle to dominate Chicago's bootleg kingdom.

Nugent was considered a vicious killer with the machine gun, as was fellow Rat member Fred Burke. In fact, officials in Hamilton County, Ohio, are convinced that Burke and Nugent were two of the robbers who killed

Pete Dumele, the marshal of North College Hill, just a few days before the American Express robbery and Toledo murder of Officer Zientara. The two gunmen were never caught for either of the Ohio murders; however, Fred Burke was captured in 1929 near St. Joseph, Michigan, where he had gunned down a patrolman with his Tommy gun—a gun that some crime historians believe to be the very same gun that killed Officer Zientara in Toledo and was later used in the St. Valentine's Day killings. Raymond "Craneneck" Nugent also saw his shadowy career come to a gruesome end in 1931 when it was reported through the underworld that while living near Miami, he had double-crossed someone and was escorted to the Everglades and fed to the alligators.

TOLEDO: THE CRIMINAL'S REST STOP

Other notorious underworld characters of the Depression era also found their way to the banks of the Maumee River. With Toledo's geographic location in the center of so many other major cities—Detroit, Cleveland, Chicago and Cincinnati—it was always believed that Toledo was a crossroads, a middle ground of sorts and a neutral territory for the big gangs and bootleggers. It was a place where they could come to enjoy themselves or meet with little interference from local law enforcement that was mostly friendly and passive.

It is often mentioned in Toledo that Al "Scarface" Capone used to make regular stops in Toledo and would hang out at the Stork's Nest Club on Bancroft, a saloon and gambling parlor where men could find a woman of easy virtue. It was in the rural countryside back then, and behind the place is where Capone and his henchmen would practice shooting their machine guns and other firearms. True? Hard to prove, but it has always made for an interesting story, and the current owners of the restaurant proudly tell the tale on the back of their menu.

One of the more unusual characters of the gangster era who found his way to Toledo and never returned was Dr. Joe Moran. He was a Chicago doctor who ran into trouble with the medical board for drinking too much and with the law for performing abortions. He lost his license and did time at a state prison in Illinois, where he met some men who thought they could use his services when he got out. So Dr. Moran started helping underworld types as a personal emergency room doctor, bandaging cuts, removing bullets

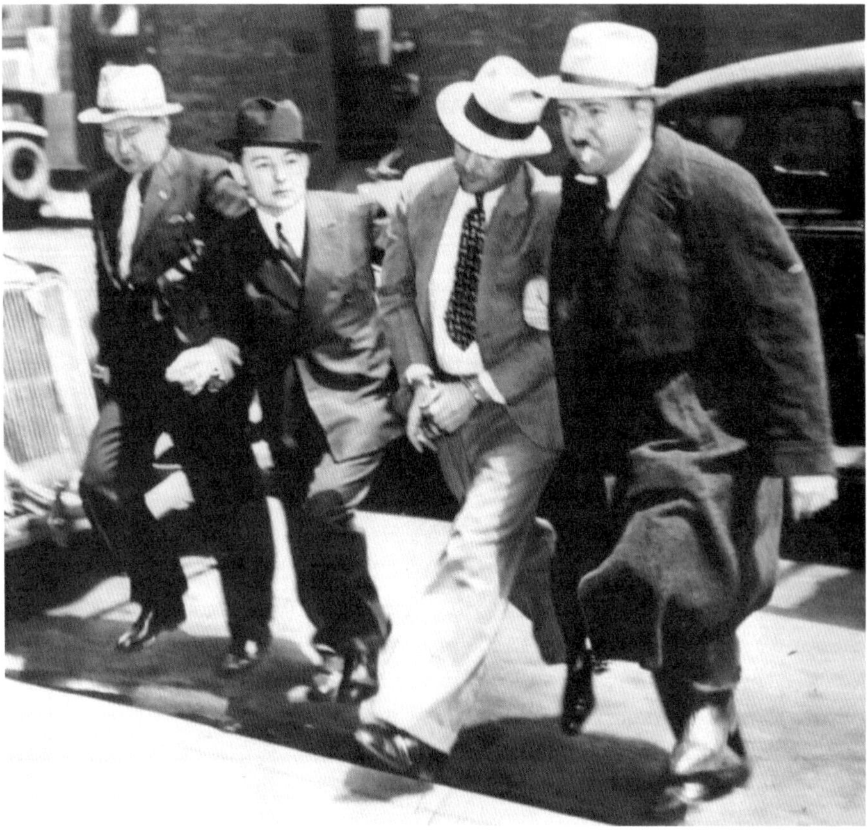

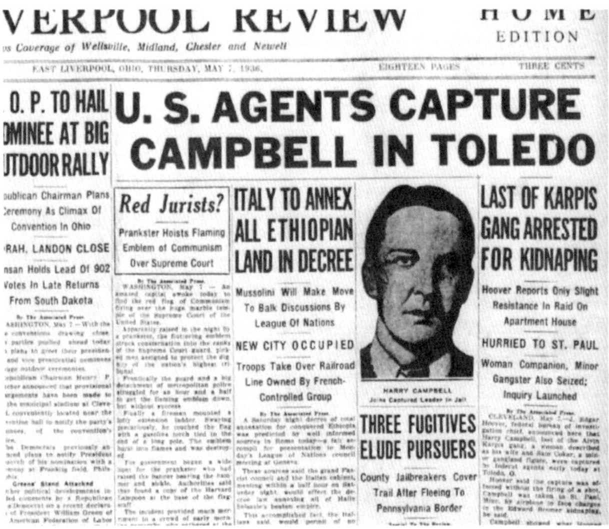

VERPOOL REVIEW

HOME EDITION

...s Coverage of Wellsville, Midland, Chester and Newell

EAST LIVERPOOL, OHIO, THURSDAY, MAY 7, 1936. EIGHTEEN PAGES THREE CENTS

U. S. AGENTS CAPTURE CAMPBELL IN TOLEDO

.O. P. TO HAIL ...OMINEE AT BIG ...UTDOOR RALLY

...publican Chairman Plans ...Ceremony As Climax Of Convention In Ohio

...RAH, LANDON CLOSE

...nsan Holds Lead Of 902 Votes In Late Returns From South Dakota

Red Jurists?

Prankster Hoists Flaming Emblem of Communism Over Supreme Court

ITALY TO ANNEX ALL ETHIOPIAN LAND IN DECREE

Mussolini Will Make Move To Balk Discussions By League Of Nations

NEW CITY OCCUPIED

Troops Take Over Railroad Line Owned By French-Controlled Group

HARRY CAMPBELL

LAST OF KARPIS GANG ARRESTED FOR KIDNAPING

Hoover Reports Only Slight Resistance In Raid On Apartment House

HURRIED TO ST. PAUL

Woman Companion, Minor Gangster Also Seized; Inquiry Launched

THREE FUGITIVES ELUDE PURSUERS

County Jailbreakers Cover Trail After Fleeing To Pennsylvania Border

Above: Harry Campbell being escorted by G-men into Cleveland federal court after his arrest in Toledo, May 1936. *Photo by* Toledo Blade.

Left: Campbell's surprise arrest in Toledo fueled sensational headlines throughout the nation. *From* East Liverpool Review.

or stitching wounds. Moran, by the 1930s, began offering plastic surgery services, changing fingerprints or altering facial features. In July 1934, while residing in Toledo to work on some members of the Barker Karpis gang, which was laying low in Toledo, he let the bravado of alcohol take over his brain and began talking too loudly, boasting to his underworld clients that he knew so much he could put them all in jail. "I got you all in the palm of my hand," he bragged. Dr. Joseph P. Moran was taken for a moonlight fishing trip that night on Lake Erie. His body would float to the southern shore of Canada a few months later, minus hands and feet. He would brag no more. (Alvin Karpis later denied this and said Dr. Moran had been buried in a lime pit in Michigan.)

THE NIGHT THAT J. EDGAR CAME TO TOLEDO

But in the end, it didn't matter what Dr. Moran knew about the Karpis gang and their hide-out in Toledo, for the FBI had other sources, and after an intensive methodical investigation, J. Edgar Hoover, the top G-man himself, came to Toledo one night and made headlines and history.

By the early 1930s, Toledo was gang-infested. Some came here to make money and trouble; others came to cool their heels and quietly hang out. Such was the story with the Karpis Barker gang, a confederacy of crime headed by Alvin "Creepy" Karpis and Fred Barker, both from the Oklahoma area, who met while doing time in a Tulsa jail. After getting out, they teamed up and conspired to rob banks and pull off kidnappings. Along the way, Karpis picked up Harry Campbell, often called "Limpy" because he had a bad leg. He was yet another small-time thief and robber with bigger aspirations. There were a gaggle of other disciples in this band of bad men, including, of course, the notorious "Ma Barker," Fred's mother, who some contend was the gang's mastermind, while others counter that such a characterization of her as the gang leader was pure fiction. After a year of forcefully stealing money from store clerks and bank depositors across the Midwest and leaving blood and bodies along the trail, Barker-Karpis cohorts were convinced they should lay low for a while in the Minneapolis area, where the police were believed to be "easy" on gangs. Criminal ambitions never take a long holiday, so it was soon after their arrival in Minnesota that Alvin Karpis decided to enter the higher-stakes world of kidnap-for-ransom. The first victim to be plucked off the streets was William Hamm, the brewing magnate. They netted $100,000 for his ransom and got away with it. Then it was Edward Bremmer, a Minnesota banker, who became their next target. Another jackpot ransom of $200,000 in cash. They released Bremmer unharmed and had their money but were now the hunted prey of a massive manhunt by the FBI. Karpis was declared Public Enemy Number One. Pictures of the cold-eyed, snarled-lip "Creepy" Karpis, Doc and Fred Barker and the limping Harry Campbell were everywhere, from post offices to newspapers to true crime magazines. They had made it to the center ring of the American criminal circus.

Karpis and Campbell managed to escape the Minnesota dragnet of lawmen and eventually, after several close calls and a shoot-out with police in Atlantic City, found their way to Toledo. They were hot targets but felt somewhat comfortable in the city, as Toledo had a reputation as a place where local law enforcement was itself corrupt and made for an easy hiding spot. In the FBI's declassified vault of case files, a riveting tale is found of the gang's movements in the Toledo area as Campbell, Karpis and other members of the gang tried to stay out of sight and blend in. Campbell, Karpis and some of the gang members were staying first at a place on Edgewater Drive in Point Place in 1934, but as the FBI got wind of it and was about to raid the place, Karpis and Campbell were tipped off and fled. They would later return to Toledo and spend much of their time at a house of ill repute on Southard Avenue, a few blocks from the Safety Building Police Station. They were put up as roomers by Edith Barry and became "friendly" with some of the girls. They also spent time with a man and wife who ran another house on Adams Street. It was a so-called house of assignation, where rooms were rented by the hour as a place for couples to have privacy. Harry Campbell must have found Toledo an agreeable place to rest easy because, using the fake name of "Bob Miller," he often went for walks, frequented local clubs and got to know some of the local gangsters who ran the gambling halls and nightclubs.

His two years in Toledo, however, were not entirely without more criminal inspiration. In 1935, Campbell and Karpis planned yet another big robbery—one that Karpis hoped would net more than $400,000. The object was a mail train, and in November 1935, they plotted and robbed the train at Garretsville, Ohio, in Portage County. The getaway plan was complex and utilized the skills of some local underworld types, like Toledo's gambling king Joe Roscoe and bootlegger and pilot John Zetzer of Port Clinton. They took the stolen mail bags to Zetzer's garage in Port Clinton, and the next morning, Zetzer flew Alvin Karpis to Arkansas. Another gang member was flown on to Oklahoma. Harry Campbell stayed behind and made his way back to Toledo, where he had a wife waiting. Her name was Gertrude, and earlier in 1935, using his assumed name of "Bob Miller," they had married and lived for a while in a camping trailer at Gertrude's mother's home until the weather turned cold. After the mail train robbery in November, they moved into an apartment in the 2100 block of Monroe Street as Bob and Gertrude Miller. Mrs. Miller had no idea who she was really married to and sharing her life with.

By 1936, prohibition was over, and with the Licavoli gang taken off the streets, the torrent of violent crime had calmed somewhat, but gambling and prostitution were still running rampant and openly. It was reported that as many as fifty houses of prostitution were operating in the city, with the owners making regular payoffs to government officials and police. The FBI agents noted this passive attitude by police as they began their work in Toledo. It was one of the reasons that the FBI did not inform local police that surveillance agents were quietly watching, tapping phone lines and doing interviews. Another reason was that they, too, had noted what appeared to be a friendly acquaintance between fugitive Harry Campbell and Lucas County sheriff James O'Reilly. O'Reilly was often seen in the company of "Bob Miller," as they met at the Goulet Grille next door to Campbell's Monroe Street apartment. Sheriff O'Reilly even helped Campbell get a pet dog from a local kennel. Did the sheriff know who "Bob Miller" really was? He said until his dying day that he did not. He had never seen a picture of Campbell, and he had no idea that his new "friend" was one of the most wanted men in America.

But one woman did know, or at least had a good hunch. She was a neighbor to the "Millers" on Monroe Street, and when Mrs. Fosnaught caught a glimpse of some of the suspicious characters coming and going from the apartment, it set off alarms that something was not right. She also noted that Bob Miller looked a lot like Harry Campbell, the fugitive whose picture she had seen in a magazine. The FBI had been closing in on the Barker Karpis gang for several years, and many of them had already been captured or killed, including Ma Barker and her son Fred, who had been killed in a shoot-out with the FBI in Florida the previous year. If Harry Campbell was aware that the FBI was on to his whereabouts and was tailing his every move, his actions didn't seem to show it. He was still going about life as normal, probably living off proceeds of the train robbery.

On May 1, 1938, the end was at hand. Federal agents finally nabbed Campbell's cohort in crime, Alvin "Creepy" Karpis, who was captured and arrested personally by FBI director J. Edgar Hoover in New Orleans. It was big news, and it left Harry Campbell as the last one of the gang still free—but not for long. In the early morning hours of May 7, 1936, a plane landed at Toledo's Transcontinental Airport, and among the fedora-topped army of G-men that disembarked was J. Edgar Hoover himself. Four carloads of heavily armed agents drove up to the apartment house in the 2100 block of Monroe Street, and according to witnesses, they started "clambering" all over the building and blocked any possible escape. Somebody banged on the door to the apartment and shouted, "Open up, Miller." Gertrude, his wife, answered the door. The FBI agents went to the bedroom where Harry was asleep. Hoover lifted the blanket and said, "Harry, time to get up, it's over." Soon, Harry Campbell was being led out of the apartment in hand and leg shackles. Gertrude was in tears as she was learning who she was married to. Mrs. Fosnaught, the woman who lived next door, trembled as she watched the scene unfold. She admitted to newspaper reporters that she had been suspicious of the couple in apartment 1.

J. Edgar Hoover talked to reporters briefly and told them he thought Campbell and Karpis were "yellow" and they were "rats" for the crimes they had committed. He also told the press he didn't think that Gertrude, Campbell's "pretty young wife," had any clue who her husband really was or what he did. It was also revealed to his wife that morning that Campbell wasn't just wanted for robberies and kidnapping but was also wanted for the murder of a lawyer in Tulsa, Oklahoma. The twenty-year-old Gertrude was released from custody to live with the shock of this revelation.

The city of Toledo was also shocked by the news that a high-profile gangster had been living among them for two years, right under their noses, and that the police not only were unaware but that the sheriff had actually been friendly with Campbell. Calls for O'Reilly's resignation were immediate, coming from the public and the press. The *Blade* called for him to step down the next day. O'Reilly, who admitted his friendship with Campbell, said he just never knew who he was. "Had I known who he was, he would have been behind bars long ago," the sheriff told a reporter in his defense, although it was pointed out that Campbell's wanted poster was on the department bulletin board for months before the arrest. The Toledo Police Department was also taking heat for not being aware of the investigation, and the public wanted to know why. Police Chief Ray Allen fired off a letter to J. Edgar Hoover wanting to know why Toledo police were kept in the dark and not informed of the impending raid on Campbell's apartment. In the FBI vault files, Hoover is quoted as saying that the Toledo Police Department couldn't

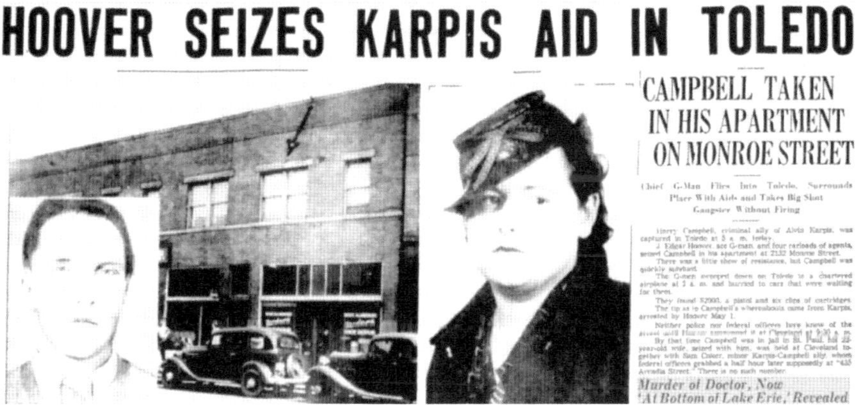

HOOVER SEIZES KARPIS AID IN TOLEDO

CAMPBELL TAKEN IN HIS APARTMENT ON MONROE STREET

Chief G-Man Flies Into Toledo, Surrounds Place With Aids and Takes Big Shot Gangster Without Firing

Murder of Doctor, Now 'At Bottom of Lake Erie,' Revealed

Toledo News Bee front page, May 7, 1936. The city was shocked that the Karpis gang had been hiding in Toledo.

be trusted. Publicly, he stated, "I said I would not cooperate with any police department that was corrupt, inefficient or publicity mad." It was a stinging indictment against the TPD and the Sheriff's Office and signaled the start of some reforms, although open gambling and prostitution would flourish for at least another decade in Toledo, and Toledo's reputation as a gang haven would become a focus of congressional hearings by the 1950s.

For the FBI, the arrest of Harry Campbell signaled the end of the long and bloody American gangster era of the Great Depression. From 1931 to 1935, the FBI and other agencies had either arrested or killed all of the nation's top outlaws who had been menacing the streets. Capone was behind bars; Licavoli was in jail; Dillinger was dead, and so, too, were Ma Barker and Bonnie and Clyde, as were many others who dared to flaunt their criminal hubris in the face of the law. The list is long and includes many who had at one time or another found their way to the "gangster junction" of Toledo.

CHAPTER 20

TOLEDO'S FIRST NATIVE SON

Man of Money and Mystery

If you're from East Toledo or have traveled there, you've probably seen a little city park known as Prentice Park. It's not a very big park, just a small triangle of grass a block off Woodville Road, bounded by Elmore, Leonard and Prentice Streets. You may know that it is Toledo's oldest city park and is named in honor of Frederick Prentice, the first white child born in what would become the city of Toledo. But what you may not know is that this early Toledo pioneer would one day become a wealthy man of influence and affluence. One of Toledo's first millionaires, he was a fascinating figure of our history whose long résumé includes experiences as a lumberman, a nurseryman, an oilman, a land speculator, a mine operator and at one time an Indian interpreter. Over the course of his nine decades of life, he married four times, had four children and left a legacy that is still in existence on many streets of America. If that's not enough, Prentice also occupies center stage in a lost treasure legend on Lake Superior.

The amazing story of Frederick Prentice begins in 1822, when he was born in the first wood-frame house in an area of what was then called Port Lawrence, at a location not far from today's Monroe and Summit Streets. The Prentice family lived near the banks of the Maumee and Swan Creek when the area was still wilderness and populated by Indians. Young Prentice, as a boy, learned their language and became fluent in its use, enough so that he was called to serve as an interpreter for traders and Indian agents in the area. In fact, it was Prentice who gave Swan Creek its name, claiming that's what the Indians called the creek because swans came there to nest.

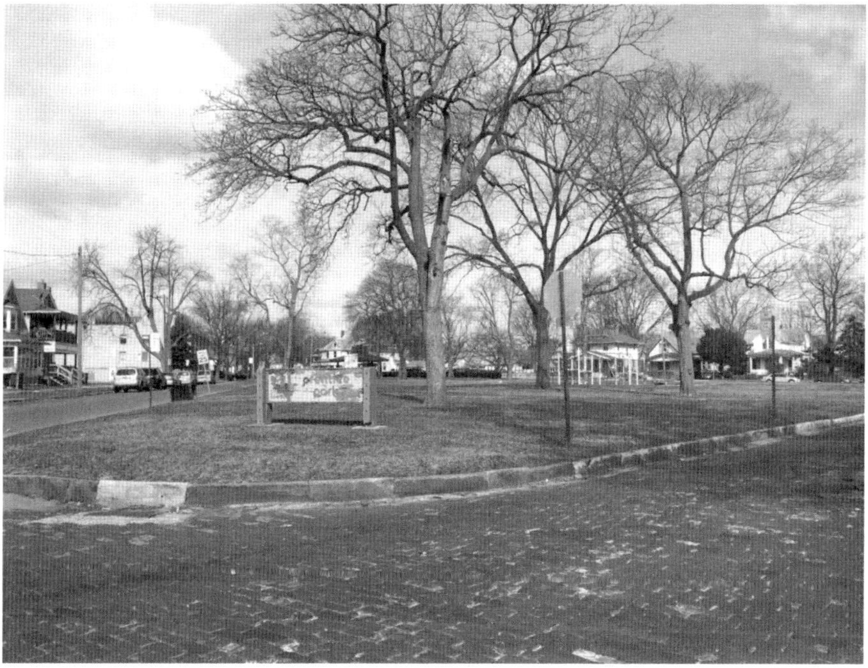

Prentice Park in East Toledo. *Author's collection.*

By the time Frederick was thirteen, his father, Joseph Prentice, credited with building the famous "blockhouse" used in the city's official seal and flag, had moved his family to the east side of the Maumee River, not far from today's town of Rossford. But the elder Prentice became disabled, and that forced young Frederick to provide for his mother and other siblings. He adapted quickly to the challenge. He hunted and fished for food, and within a few years, Prentice started buying and selling local land to people coming to the area. In 1838, he started his own sawmill along the banks of the Maumee River. It was a successful enterprise that met the growing demand for lumber for homes and shipbuilding. Business was good for the young man who, without any formal education, quickly reached for other opportunities and expanded his business ventures. He farmed and also started a tree nursery in East Toledo, at the same time also buying more land to meet the demands of the land speculation frenzy. He did so not just in Toledo but as far away as the northern woods of Wisconsin and the Minnesota Territory, where he and other investors set up logging operations and platted several towns along Lake Superior. The land was cheap, and he figured it might be worth much more in the future. He was right.

Frederick A. Prentice was the true definition of an entrepreneur: smart, clever and shrewd. Quick to answer the knock of opportunity, his enterprising spirit did not go unrewarded. He became prosperous and wealthy while still a young man. His success earned the respect of others in Toledo, which by the mid-1800s had become a city of great promise on the Great Lakes. Despite a financial setback by the financial Panic of 1857, Prentice was able to recover within a few years and renewed his quest for fortune. In doing so, he recognized the need for oil and bought holdings in the new and burgeoning petroleum industry in Pennsylvania. The investments were lucrative, and by the 1870s, he was living and working in New York City, while still maintaining a house on North Summit Street in Toledo. At the same time, he was looking to the north for future projects.

One of those opportunities was in sandstone excavation to meet the need for building blocks being utilized in America's cities. He put together an investment partnership in some brownstone quarry property that he had purchased years before in northern Wisconsin, along Lake Superior in the Apostle Islands. Soon, the Prentice Brownstone Quarry Company was removing hundreds of thousands of tons of brownstone from these quarries and shipping the giant blocks to projects in New York City, Buffalo, Cleveland and Cincinnati. The brownstone was also used in Chicago, a city still rebuilding after the Great Fire of 1871. The colorful stone is still visible today on some landmark buildings in Chicago and other cities, including the Palmer House Hotel in Chicago and Cincinnati City Hall.

One of the quarries that Prentice took this stone from was the Excelsior Quarry on Hermit Island in Lake Superior, part of what is now called the Apostle Islands. It was a prolific producer of brownstone and employed at least one hundred men who took hundreds of thousands of tons of stone from the quarry to be shipped around the nation. Prentice loved the small rugged island, which was said to be haunted by a man named Wilson who once lived and was murdered there. That tale didn't discourage Prentice, who wanted to live there with his new bride from New York. So the romantic and often flamboyant Prentice built a mansion of sorts on Hermit Island: a giant three-story lakefront home that featured Romeo and Juliet balconies, four fireplaces carved of brownstone and an observation tower. The house was clad with a rustic-looking cedar bark shingle. Thus, he called his island mansion the Cedar Bark Cottage, and in 1891, he proudly escorted his young wife, Lydia Amanda, to Hermit Island to see her new home. Exactly what was said and what happened is unknowable at this point, but it's reported that when the young Manhattan-bred lady saw the rustic cedar bark exterior, she turned and walked away and never returned. Locals believe it was the ghostly presence of the old man Wilson who didn't want a woman to move onto his island that made Lydia dislike the place. Others thought she was just spoiled. In any event, Prentice's hopes were crushed. He did open the house for tours and even entertained the Wisconsin governor there, along with other dignitaries, but soon the proud home sat empty and abandoned. The harsh winter winds on Lake Superior were proficient in the task of beating up the home beyond repair, as holes were torn in the roof and doors came off hinges. What nature didn't reclaim and destroy, vandals did, and within a few decades, the Cedar Bark Cottage was in shambles.

What notions the Toledo native may have had about a marriage of lakefront bliss would have been dealt a body blow anyway with the stock market Panic of 1893. The brakes were put on the economy, and the market for brownstone crashed. The big quarries were idled, and the big blocks of brown sandstone were left untouched. Many still remain, to this day, numbered and waiting for the ships that never came to take them away.

Another dream of Frederick Prentice's was also toppled with the quaking economy. In 1892, Prentice and the Wisconsin governor were talking about the quality of the stone from the quarries, and Prentice bragged that he could cut the largest monolith ever in one piece from his Hermit Island quarry and have it lifted and shipped out for the upcoming World's Fair in Chicago. The governor saw this as a good way to promote Wisconsin and said the state would pay for the shipping. It was a tall order, as the monolith would have to be at least 110 feet tall and would weigh tons. But true to his word, Prentice put a crew of men on the project and had them cut an obelisk 115 feet tall and 10 feet wide at the base, tapering to 4 feet at the top. He was able to get it cut and separated and ready to be shipped. The World's Fair was waiting, but by 1893, as the markets fell and the cost of shipping the stone grew to more than $25,000, the State of Wisconsin backed out on its pledge. The world's largest monolith would never leave the quarry. The four-hundred-ton stone was soon cut up and used for other projects. But it was not to disappoint fairgoers. By the time the fair opened, Prentice had four 25-foot monuments made of brownstone shipped there. They included a Wisconsin badger, a life-sized statue of a Chippewa chief and the heads of African Americans carved in bas-relief. The fairgoers were greeted with Wisconsin brownstone throughout the fairgrounds. It was a proud moment for Prentice, but then the future of stone began to crumble for the Toledo millionaire.

The quarry operations went bankrupt, Cedar Bark Cottage was torn down, he sold his property on the island and his days in Upper Wisconsin were numbered. What does remain of the legend of the "brownstone king" and the name of Toledo's first child? In nearby Washburn, Wisconsin, townsfolk built their own miniature version (one-quarter scale) of Prentice's brownstone obelisk in his honor. They even call Washburn the "Monolith City," and the twenty-seven-foot tower still stands. If you're ever visiting that area, you can see it, and you might also want to check out Prentice Park in Ashland, Wisconsin, the "Park of a Hundred Springs." This is a park that Prentice purchased from the Chippewa Indians in 1887. It is filled with scores of natural-flowing artesian wells and is run by the City of Ashland. The Prentice name is also familiar to an army of latter-day treasure hunters who continue to fuel a stubborn myth of the "hermit" on the Hermit Island many years later and that it was Prentice himself who buried his fortune, in cash, near the Cedar Bark Cottage. As a result, it's not hard to find references to Toledo's Prentice on several fortune hunter websites as romantic dreamers peddle this shaky tale, luring folks with shovels and metal detectors to the island every year in search of the Prentice fortune. The fact is that Prentice lost the quarries and Hermit Island to foreclosure auction during bankruptcy action by 1900. He never returned.

What helps to fuel this stubborn myth is the lack of knowledge about Frederick Prentice's final years. For all practical purposes, after the big quarries shut down, he seems to have slipped back into relative obscurity. It does appear that he returned to New York City, but little is written about this figure who was no stranger to the press and who relished the art of living large. What we do know is that Frederick Prentice died in April 1913 at the age of ninety-two. Where he died and whether he still had his wealth remain murky at best. A newspaper account from the *Toledo News Bee* says he died on his "estate" on the Hudson River. But a Prentice family website says he died in Jackson, Michigan. In the 1910 census for New York, the entry shows him living as a "boarder" with his wife, Lydia, in upper Manhattan. She was his fourth wife and died in 1912. But neither she nor his third wife, Mary, is buried with him at Willow Cemetery in Oregon in the Prentice family plot that includes his parents; his daughter, Mary; and his first two wives. Prentice has a marker at Willow, but it's generally believed that it is only a memorial and his remains rest somewhere in New York along the Hudson River. We may never know for sure. What we do know, however, is that the story of Frederick Prentice is one that is rich, colorful and mysterious—the story of a man who is worthy of more than a mere footnote in Toledo's history and a small unmarked park in East Toledo.

Index

About the Author

Lou Hebert is a northwest Ohio native, having grown up in the rural world of corn fields and lime plants in western Ottawa County. His passion for history and his professional experience as a broadcast journalist for five decades have inspired him to read more old newspapers than new ones, researching and chronicling the colorful events and characters that populate the forgotten past of the old Back Swamp. Lou was formally educated at the University of Toledo and Bowling Green State University but earned his advanced degrees in life from the many "professors" he met in bars, poolrooms, police stations, street corners and factories where listening with a keen ear was the only cost of tuition. Lou's vigor for finding and telling stories has taken him to many corners of the country over the decades, working in an atlas of cities and states. He spent about fifteen years in the Colorado area as a TV and radio reporter. Eventually, Lou returned home to Toledo, where he has discovered the area's past to be as rich and robust as any city in the nation. His talents as a broadcast storyteller have netted him numerous awards and honors, including several Emmy Awards, AP Awards and a coveted John Foster Peabody Award from the University of Georgia for investigative documentary production. Besides writing, Lou is an avid reader and loves the beauty and treasure of nature, writing music and, when he has free time, playing golf as badly as he plays the guitar. He has five sons and a very understanding and tolerant wife.